ENGLISH/SPANISH
INGLÉS/ESPAÑOL

THE BASIC OXFORD

Picture Dictionary

Second Edition

MARGOT F. GRAMER

Translated by Sergio Gaitán

OXFORD
UNIVERSITY PRESS

OXFORD
UNIVERSITY PRESS

198 Madison Avenue
New York, NY 10016 USA

Great Clarendon Street
Oxford OX2 6DP England

Oxford New York

Auckland Cape Town Dar es Salaam Hong Kong Karachi
Kuala Lumpur Madrid Melbourne Mexico City Nairobi
New Delhi Shanghai Taipei Toronto

With offices in

Argentina Austria Brazil Chile Czech Republic France Greece
Guatemala Hungary Italy Japan Poland Portugal Singapore
South Korea Switzerland Thailand Turkey Ukraine Vietnam

OXFORD is a trademark of Oxford University Press.

ISBN : 978 0 19 437235 0

Copyright © 2003 Oxford University Press

Library of Congress Cataloging-in-Publication Data
Gramer, Margot.
   [Basic Oxford picture dictionary. Spanish & English]
   The basic Oxford picture dictionary / Margot F. Gramer; translated
   by Sergio Gaitán—English / Spanish ed., 2nd ed.
      p. cm.
   Includes index.
   ISBN: 978 0 19 437235 0

1. Picture dictionaries, Spanish. 2. Picture dictionaries, English.
3. Spanish language—Dictionaries—English. 4. English language—
Dictionaries—Spanish. I. Title
   PC4629.G7313 2003   463'.21—dc21   2002070372

No unauthorized photocopying.

All rights reserved. No part of this publication may be reproduced, stored
in a retrieval system, or transmitted, in any form or by any means, electronic,
mechanical, photocopying, recording, or otherwise, without the prior written
permission of Oxford University Press.

This book is sold subject to the condition that it shall not, by way of trade
or otherwise, be lent, resold, hired out, or otherwise circulated without the
publisher's prior consent in any form of binding or cover other than that in
which it is published and without a similar condition including this condition
being imposed on the subsequent purchaser.

Illustrations: Wendy Wassink Ackion, Skip Baker, Mary Chandler,
Steven Chorney, Graphic Chart & Map Co., International Mapping Associates,
Karen Loccisano, Laura Hartman Maestro, Yoshi Miyake, Rob Schuster,
Joel Snyder, Don Stewart, Anna Vitfort

Icons by Stephan Van Litsenborg

"To the Teacher" translated by Booklinks Publishing Services

Editorial Manager: Janet Aitchison
Project Manager: Amy Cooper
Senior Production Editor: Jeff Holt
Production Editor: Stephanie Ruiz
Senior Designer: Mary Chandler
Layout Artist: Jennifer Manzelli
Senior Art Buyer: Jodi Waxman
Production Manager: Shanta Persaud
Production Coordinator: Eve Wong

Cover Concept: Silver Editions
Cover Illustrations: Craig Attebury, Jin DeLapine, Narda Lebo,
Mohammad Mansoor, Tom Newsom, Bill Thomson

Printing (last digit): 10 9 8 7 6 5

Printed in Hong Kong.

Acknowledgements

Oxford University Press gratefully acknowledges the work of the teachers and administrators who helped to shape this book:

Jayme Adelson-Goldstein, Los Angeles Unified School District

Fiona Armstrong, New York City Board of Education

Shirley Brod, Spring Institute for International Studies

Ann Creighton, Los Angeles Unified School District

Irene Frankel, The New School for Social Research

Rheta Goldman, North Hollywood Adult Learning Center

Jean Pilger, New York City Board of Education

Norma Shapiro, Los Angeles Unified School District

Kathleen Santopietro Weddel, Consultant, Northern Colorado State Literacy Resource Center

Renée Weiss, North Hollywood Adult Learning Center

Our special thanks to Jayme Adelson-Goldstein, Fiona Armstrong, and Norma Shapiro, who served as *Dictionary* consultants and wrote the accompanying *Teacher's Resource Book of Reproducible Activities, Workbook,* and *Picture Cards*. Ms. Adelson-Goldstein and Ms. Shapiro also wrote the *Teacher's Book*. The deep commitment of the authors to student-centered learning played a critical role in the development of *The Basic Oxford Picture Dictionary Program*.

To the Teacher   Al Maestro

El programa del Basic Oxford Dictionary

El programa del Basic Oxford Dictionary fue diseñado para atender las necesidades de los estudiantes jóvenes y adultos de nivel principiante, entre ellos los de nivel básico de lecto-escritura. Este programa cubre las necesidades básicas de los estudiantes de ESL y EFL e incluye práctica de las cuatro destrezas de una manera flexible. *El Basic Oxford Picture Dictionary* es el componente base, en el que se presenta el vocabulario clave en contexto de una manera visual y completa. Este vocabulario se considera necesario para que un estudiante de nivel principiante pueda desenvolverse en la vida diaria. Por sí solo, el *Dictionary* es un material didáctico muy valioso. Junto con sus otros componentes, los *Cassettes, Teacher's Book, Teacher's Resource Book of Reproducible Activities* and *Cassette* (libro de recursos del maestro con páginas de actividades reproducibles y casetes), *Workbook* (cuaderno de práctica), *Picture Cards* (juego de tarjetas ilustradas), *Transparencies* (transparencias) y el *Literacy Program* (programa de lecto-escritura), el *Dictionary* forma un programa de enseñanza de idiomas completo.

El Basic Oxford Picture Dictionary, Second Edition

El Basic Oxford Picture Dictionary, Second Edition tiene varias nuevas características importantes que hacen que el *Dictionary* sea aún más accesible y útil para los estudiantes de nivel principiante y sus maestros:

- Cada tema incluye ejercicios fáciles que ofrecen la oportunidad de practicar el vocabulario nuevo.

- La guía codificada con colores facilita la identificación de los temas.

- Se han cambiado algunas de las ilustraciones para reflejar un estilo más moderno.

- El *Teacher's Book* nuevo incluye *El Basic Oxford Picture Dictionary, Second Edition* completo. Las notas del margen ofrecen planes de lecciones paso a paso, estrategias de enseñanza, ideas creativas para ampliar las sesiones de clase y notas culturales.

Es importante resaltar que *El Basic Oxford Picture Dictionary, Second Edition* tiene las mismas características clave que hicieron que la primera edición fuera tan popular: un diseño de página claro, un tipo de letra grande y fácil de leer y un número limitado de palabras por página. Las 1,200 palabras y frases de uso frecuente—un vocabulario que es útil en la vida diaria de los estudiantes jóvenes o adultos—son las mismas que en la edición anterior. El vocabulario se presenta en ilustraciones a todo color, que muestran cada palabra en un contexto de la vida real. El *Dictionary* está dividido en 12 áreas temáticas distintas. Sin embargo, se puede usar en cualquier orden, según las necesidades de los estudiantes.

Para que haya claridad, se incluye el nombre más común de cada concepto. (Cuando existen dos palabras para un mismo concepto, a menudo se incluyen ambas.) Los sustantivos, los adjetivos y las preposiciones se identifican con un número; los verbos se identifican con una letra. A su vez, las ilustraciones están numeradas consecutivamente, de izquierda a derecha y de arriba a abajo, cuando es posible.

El índice y la guía de pronunciación del Apéndice facilitan la localización de las palabras y la pronunciación correcta de una manera fácil y rápida. Un conjunto completo de *Dictionary Cassettes* ofrece la oportunidad de escuchar todas las palabras del *Dictionary*.

Cómo usar El Basic Oxford Picture Dictionary, Second Edition de manera efectiva

El Basic Oxford Picture Dictionary, Second Edition es el material didáctico ideal para los estudiantes de nivel principiante y los que están aprendiendo a leer. Las sugerencias que siguen ofrecen instrucciones para usar *El Basic Oxford Picture Dictionary* de una manera efectiva en una clase comunicativa. Si necesita más sugerencias para usarlo en la clase, vea *El Basic Oxford Picture Dictionary Teacher's Book* y el *Teacher's Resource Book of Reproducible Activities.*

1. Seleccione un tema que cubra las necesidades de los estudiantes.

Los 68 temas que aparecen en las páginas de Contenido reflejan las necesidades básicas de los estudiantes de nivel principiante. Al elegir un tema, considere la naturaleza de la clase, así como las necesidades inmediatas de sus estudiantes. Si desea, puede incluir a sus estudiantes en este proceso, pidiéndoles que se fijen en la Tabla de Contenido y que digan qué temas les interesan. Los temas están presentados en 12 áreas temáticas, pero usted puede reagruparlos en unidades o temas apropiados para sus estudiantes. Por ejemplo, puede elegir Vegetables de la página 34, Cooking a Meal de la página 46 y A Birthday Party de la página 17, para dar una clase sobre comida para una ocasión especial.

2. Presente el tema.

Pida a los estudiantes que se fijen en la página del *Dictionary* que haya seleccionado o en la *Overhead Transparency* correspondiente. Antes de que comiencen a practicar la palabra nueva, relacione el tema con sus vidas y permita que escuchen la palabra en un contexto de palabras que conozcan. Puede pedirles que se fijen en la página y que digan qué palabras conocen. También podrían participar en una lluvia de ideas sobre otras palabras conocidas que estén relacionadas con el tema. A su vez, usted podría describir la ilustración de manera sencilla, usando algunas palabras que conozcan, y después hacerles preguntas. Por ejemplo, para presentar la página 25, usted podría decir: *This is a kitchen. There's a woman in the kitchen. She's opening the freezer. What do you think she's taking out of the freezer? What do you think she's making?* Los gestos y las expresiones faciales pueden ayudarle a explicar el significado. Muchas de las páginas del *Dictionary* incluyen personas, así que puede preguntar a los estudiantes qué creen que están haciendo esas personas.

3. Presente las palabras de la página.

Una vez que sepa qué palabras conocen sus estudiantes, puede concentrarse en el resto de las palabras. Una manera de presentarlas es señalar la ilustración y decir la palabra. Los estudiantes pueden seguirla con usted, fijándose en las ilustraciones en sus libros a medida que usted repita este proceso para todas las palabras. Una vez que los estudiantes hayan hecho la conexión de la palabra hablada con la ilustración, pueden fijarse en la escritura escrita, a medida que usted lea cada palabra. De esta manera, los estudiantes aprenderán a relacionar el sonido de la palabra con la ilustración y con su forma escrita.

Después de la presentación inicial, puede decir una palabra al azar para que los estudiantes la señalen en la ilustración. Para comprobar que los estudiantes hayan entendido el vocabulario, camine por el salón y fíjese que señalen la ilustración correcta. Más adelante puede hacer lo contrario—señale (o haga que un estudiante señale) una ilustración y pida a los estudiantes que digan qué palabra es. También puede comprobar su compresión con preguntas, como *What is number 3?* o *What number is mop?*

4. Practiquen las palabras.

Los ejercicios de la parte de abajo de la página reforzarán las correspondencias del sonido y la palabra escrita y el sentido de las palabras a medida que los estudiantes usen el vocabulario en un contexto natural. Para ayudarlos, puede usar el vocabulario en un ejercicio antes de que los estudiantes comiencen. Los ejemplos de cada página muestran cómo se pueden usar las palabras y expresiones nuevas. Todas las palabras subrayadas en los ejemplos pueden sustituirse con otras palabras en la misma página del *Dictionary*. Al sustituir estas palabras, los estudiantes practican el vocabulario de cada página de una manera exhaustiva.

Ejercicios

- **Name** o **Talk about . . . . Point.**

El primer ejercicio de cada página generalmente requiere una identificación simple, por ejemplo, *This is a pencil,* o una descripción, por ejemplo, *There's an armchair, She's wearing a dress.* Los estudiantes dicen la oración y señalan la ilustración correspondiente en el *Dictionary*. En algunos casos, se les pide que cuenten cosas en la ilustración. En todas estas actividades, las estructuras se practican en los ejemplos y se usa un lenguaje natural en contexto.

- **Ask and answer questions.**

Existen diferentes variaciones de este ejercicio. En todas ellas, se le pide al estudiante que haga y conteste preguntas sobre las ilustraciónnes de la página. Son actividades para parejas y los papeles del diálogo se dividen en A y B. Se puede hacer este ejercicio por parejas o con toda la clase. Una mitad de la clase es A y la otra B.

- **Act it out.**

Hay algunas variaciones de esta actividad de TPR (respuesta física total). Los estudiantes tienen que representar las palabras del vocabulario e intentar adivinarlas. Los ejercicios de *Act it out* se pueden hacer en parejas o con toda la clase.

- **Talk about yourself.**

Muchas páginas incluyen este ejercicio final, en el que los estudiantes tienen la oportunidad de relacionar sus experiencias con el vocabulario. A menudo es un ejercicio para parejas, que también se puede hacer en grupos pequeños.

Notas del Lenguaje

Muchas páginas del *Dictionary* incluyen notas del lenguaje, que ofrecen más instrucciones para usar el vocabulario de manera natural. Estas anotaciones generalmente incluyen aspectos como el uso del artículo, las formas plurales y varias formas del verbo (el pasado, el presente continuo y la tercera persona del presente simple).

5. Ofrezca más práctica.

Hay numerosas sugerencias para practicar de una manera comunicativa en *El Basic Oxford Picture Dictionary Teacher's Book* y el *Teacher's Resource Book of Reproducible Activities*. Ambos ofrecen ejercicios basados en los temas del *Dictionary* y están diseñados para mejorar las destrezas de escuchar, hablar, leer, escribir y trabajar en equipo. *El Basic Oxford Picture Dictionary Workbook* presenta contextos nuevos para el vocabulario en ejercicios breves de lectura y escritura.

6. Escoja un ejercicio de aplicación.

Una vez que los estudiantes estén familiarizados con las palabras de una página o de una unidad, es importante animarlos a que usen sus conocimientos fuera del salón de clase. Algunas de las actividades que sugerimos son:

- Pida a los estudiantes que revisen en revistas, periódicos y otro tipo de publicaciones para buscar fotografías o ilustraciones del tema que están tratando.

- Pídales que entrevisten a alguien fuera de clase (un pariente o amigo), usando preguntas que incorporen el vocabulario nuevo.

- Dé los ejercicios del aplicación marcados en *El Basic Oxford Picture Dictionary Workbook* como tarea y hablen de las respuestas al día siguiente.

Contents   Contenido

pizarra/pizarrón	1. (chalk)board
gis/tiza	2. chalk
borrador	3. eraser
maestra	4. teacher
estudiante	5. student
silla	6. chair
escritorio	7. desk

libro	8. book
papel	9. paper
bolígrafo	10. pen
lápiz	11. pencil
cuaderno	12. notebook
computadora	13. computer

Language note:

a chalkboard
an eraser
a piece of chalk
a piece of paper

Name the things in the classroom. Point.

This is a pencil.
This is an eraser.

escribir	**A.** write	ver la pantalla	**H.** look at the screen
señalar	**B.** point (to)	cerrar la ventana	**I.** close the window
salir	**C.** go out	abrir un cuaderno	**J.** open a notebook
entrar	**D.** come in	levantar la mano	**K.** raise . . . hand
leer	**E.** read	conversar	**L.** talk
escuchar	**F.** listen	estar sentado	**M.** sit
trabajar con la computadora	**G.** work at the computer	estar parado	**N.** stand

A: Tell your partner what to do.
B: Act it out.

A: Please <u>raise your hand</u>.
Please <u>stand</u>.

JAN. ①

Sun.	Mon.	Tue.	Wed.	Thurs.	Fri.	Sat.
					1	2
3	4	5	6	7	8	9
10	11	12	13	14	15	16
17	18	19	20	21	22	23
24/31	25	26	27	28	29	30

FEB. ②

Sun.	Mon.	Tue.	Wed.	Thurs.	Fri.	Sat.
	1	2	3	4	5	6
7	8	9	10	11	12	13
14	15	16	17	18	19	20
21	22	23	24	25	26	27
28						

MAR. ③

Sun.	Mon.	Tue.	Wed.	Thurs.	Fri.	Sat.
	1	2	3	4	5	6
7	8	9	10	11	12	13
14	15	16	17	18	19	20
21	22	23	24	25	26	27
28	29	30	31			

APR. ④

Sun.	Mon.	Tue.	Wed.	Thurs.	Fri.	Sat.
				1	2	3
4	5	6	7	8	9	10
11	12	13	14	15	16	17
18	19	20	21	22	23	24
25	26	27	28	29	30	

MAY ⑤

Sun.	Mon.	Tue.	Wed.	Thurs.	Fri.	Sat.
						1
2	3	4	5	6	7	8
9	10	11	12	13	14	15
16	17	18	19	20	21	22
23/30	24/31	25	26	27	28	29

JUNE ⑥

Sun.	Mon.	Tue.	Wed.	Thurs.	Fri.	Sat.
		1	2	3	4	5
6	7	8	9	10	11	12
13	14	15	16	17	18	19
20	21	22	23	24	25	26
27	28	29	30			

JULY ⑦

Sun.	Mon.	Tue.	Wed.	Thurs.	Fri.	Sat.
				1	2	3
4	5	6	7	8	9	10
11	12	13	14	15	16	17
18	19	20	21	22	23	24
25	26	27	28	29	30	31

AUG. ⑧

Sun.	Mon.	Tue.	Wed.	Thurs.	Fri.	Sat.
1	2	3	4	5	6	7
8	9	10	11	12	13	14
15	16	17	18	19	20	21
22	23	24	25	26	27	28
29	30	31				

SEPT. ⑨

Sun.	Mon.	Tue.	Wed.	Thurs.	Fri.	Sat.
			1	2	3	4
5	6	7	8	9	10	11
12	13	14	15	16	17	18
19	20	21	22	23	24	25
26	27	28	29	30		

OCT. ⑩

Sun.	Mon.	Tue.	Wed.	Thurs.	Fri.	Sat.
					1	2
3	4	5	6	7	8	9
10	11	12	13	14	15	16
17	18	19	20	21	22	23
24/31	25	26	27	28	29	30

NOV. ⑪

Sun.	Mon.	Tue.	Wed.	Thurs.	Fri.	Sat.
	1	2	3	4	5	6
7	8	9	10	11	12	13
14	15	16	17	18	19	20
21	22	23	24	25	26	27
28	29	30				

DEC. ⑫

Sun.	Mon.	Tue.	Wed.	Thurs.	Fri.	Sat.
			1	2	3	4
5	6	7	8	9	10	11
12	13	14	15	16	17	18
19	20	21	22	23	24	25
26	27	28	29	30	31	

⑬

⑭

⑮

⑯

enero	1.	January
febrero	2.	February
marzo	3.	March
abril	4.	April
mayo	5.	May
junio	6.	June
julio	7.	July
agosto	8.	August
septiembre	9.	September
octubre	10.	October
noviembre	11.	November
diciembre	12.	December
invierno	13.	winter
primavera	14.	spring
verano	15.	summer
otoño	16.	fall

Talk about the months and seasons. Point.

This is _January_. It's _winter_.

Talk about yourself.

A: *Do you like _winter_?*
B: *Yes, I do. / No, I don't.*

JANUARY

① Sun.	② Mon.	③ Tue.	④ Wed.	⑤ Thurs.	⑥ Fri.	⑦ Sat.
					1 ⑧	2 ⑨
3 ⑩	4	5	6	7	8	9
10	11	12	13	14 ⑭	15	16
17	18	19	20 ⑮	21	22	23
24 / 31	25	26	27	28	29	30

⑯

	JAN.							FEB.							MAR.							APR.							MAY							JUNE				

The twelve mini-calendars show: JAN., FEB., MAR., APR., MAY, JUNE, JULY, AUG., SEPT., OCT., NOV., DEC., each with columns Sun. Mon. Tue. Wed. Thurs. Fri. Sat.

domingo	**1.** Sunday
lunes	**2.** Monday
martes	**3.** Tuesday
miércoles	**4.** Wednesday
jueves	**5.** Thursday
viernes	**6.** Friday
sábado	**7.** Saturday
primero / 1º	**8.** 1st

segundo	**9.** 2nd
tercero	**10.** 3rd
ayer	**11.** yesterday
hoy	**12.** today
mañana	**13.** tomorrow
día	**14.** day
semana	**15.** week
año	**16.** year

Talk about the calendar.

Today is <u>Wednesday</u>.
Tomorrow is _____.
Yesterday was _____.

Talk about this week. Use words 1–7.

Today is _____.
Tomorrow is _____.
Yesterday was _____.

mañana	**1.** morning
tarde	**2.** afternoon
anochecer	**3.** evening
noche	**4.** night

sol	**5.** sun
luna	**6.** moon
estrellas	**7.** stars

Talk about pictures 1–4. Point.
It's morning.

A: Ask questions.
B: Act out the answers.

A: What do you do in the morning?
*   What do you do at night?*

6

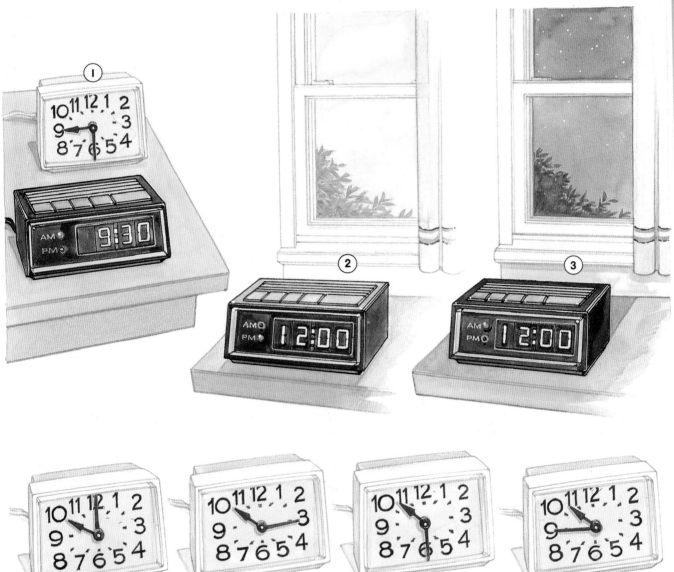

reloj	**1.** clock	
mediodía	**2.** noon	
medianoche	**3.** midnight	
las diez en punto	**4.** ten o'clock	

las diez y quince	**5.** ten fifteen
las diez y treinta	**6.** ten thirty
un cuarto	**7.** ten forty-five
para las once	

Talk about the time. Point.

It's <u>ten o'clock</u>.

A: Ask the question and point.
B: Answer.
A: What time is it?
B: It's <u>9:30</u>.

Look at page 6, pictures 1 and 3.
A: Ask questions and point.
B: Answer.
A: Is it <u>7:00 A.M.</u> or <u>7:00 P.M.</u>?
B: It's _____.

7

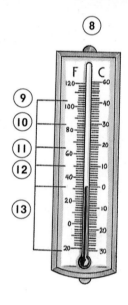

lloviendo	**1.** raining
nevando	**2.** snowing
airoso / ventoso	**3.** windy
soleado	**4.** sunny
nublado	**5.** cloudy
cubierto de hielo	**6.** icy
con neblina	**7.** foggy

temperatura	**8.** temperature
caliente	**9.** hot
cálido	**10.** warm
fresco	**11.** cool
frío	**12.** cold
congelación	**13.** freezing

Talk about pictures 1–7. Point.

It's raining.

Language note:

° = degrees; F = Fahrenheit; C = Celsius
32°F = 0°C = freezing

Ask and answer questions.

A: *How's the weather?*
B: *It's sunny and warm.*
A: *What's the temperature?*
B: *It's 82°F / 28°C.*

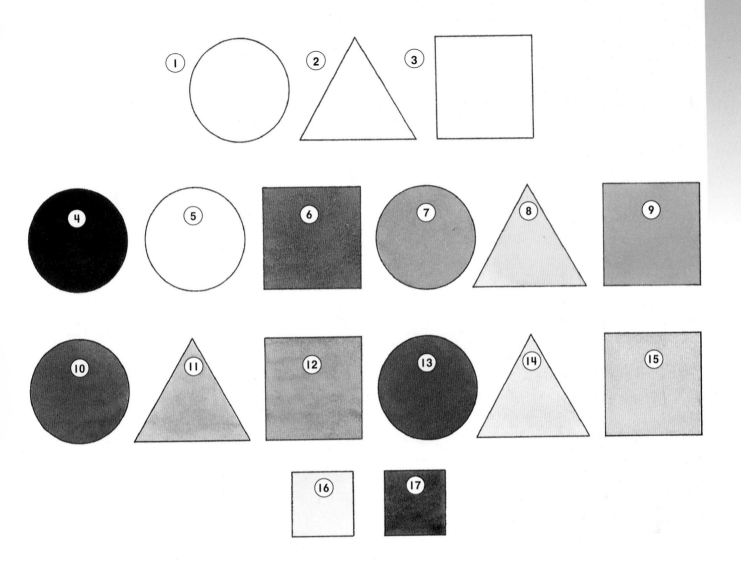

círculo	**1.** circle	
triángulo	**2.** triangle	
cuadrado	**3.** square	
negro	**4.** black	
blanco	**5.** white	
rojo	**6.** red	
azul	**7.** blue	
amarillo	**8.** yellow	
verde	**9.** green	

café	**10.** brown
gris	**11.** gray
anaranjado	**12.** orange
morado	**13.** purple
beige	**14.** beige
rosado	**15.** pink
(azul) claro	**16.** light (blue)
(azul) oscuro	**17.** dark (blue)

Name the shapes and colors. Point.

This is a white circle.
This is an orange square.

Talk about yourself.

A: *What colors do you like?*
B: *I like _____ and _____.*

9

billetes	**1.** bills
dólar	**2.** dollar
monedas	**3.** coins
centavo/ chavito prieto	**4.** penny
moneda de cinco/ vellón	**5.** nickel
moneda de diez/ sencillo	**6.** dime

moneda de veinticinco/peseta	**7.** quarter
centavos	**8.** cents
cuenta	**9.** check
factura/cuenta	**10.** bill
recibo	**11.** receipt
tarjeta de crédito	**12.** credit card

**Name the bills and coins. Point.
Use pictures 2, 4–7.**

This is a dollar.
This is a penny.

Language note:

| I nickel | 2 nickels |
| I penny | 2 pennies |

Talk about yourself.

I have a quarter and two dimes.

bebé	1. baby		hombre	5. man
niña / muchacha	2. girl		niño, niña	6. child
niño / muchacho	3. boy		adolescente	7. teenager
mujer	4. woman		adulto	8. adult

Talk about the people. Point.

She's a baby.
He's a boy.

Use the new words with pages 20–21.

A: Ask questions and point.

B: Answer.

A: *Is she a teenager?*
B: *Yes, she is.* / *No, she's an adult.*

Estatura	**Height**
alta	1. tall
de estatura media	2. average height
baja	3. short

Peso	**Weight**
pesado/gordo	4. heavy/fat
de peso medio	5. average weight
delgado/flaco	6. thin/skinny

Tamaño	**Size**
grande	7. big/large
pequeña	8. small/little

Talk about the people. Point.
She's tall.
He's heavy.

A: Ask questions and point.
B: Answer.
A: What does she look like?
B: She's small, short, and thin.

12

Pelo/Cabello	Hair		pelo/cabello rojo	18. red hair
barba	9. beard		pelo/cabello café/castaño	19. brown hair
bigote	10. mustache			
pelo/cabello largo	11. long hair		pelo/cabello negro	20. black hair
pelo/cabello corto	12. short hair		pelo/cabello gris/canoso	21. gray hair
calvo	13. bald			
pelo/cabello lacio	14. straight hair		**Edad**	**Age**
pelo/cabello ondulado	15. wavy hair		joven	22. young
			madura	23. middle-aged
pelo/cabello rizo	16. curly hair		anciana	24. old
pelo/cabello rubio	17. blond hair			

Talk about the people. Point.

He has <u>a beard</u>.
She has <u>long hair</u>.
He's <u>bald</u>.
She's <u>young</u>.

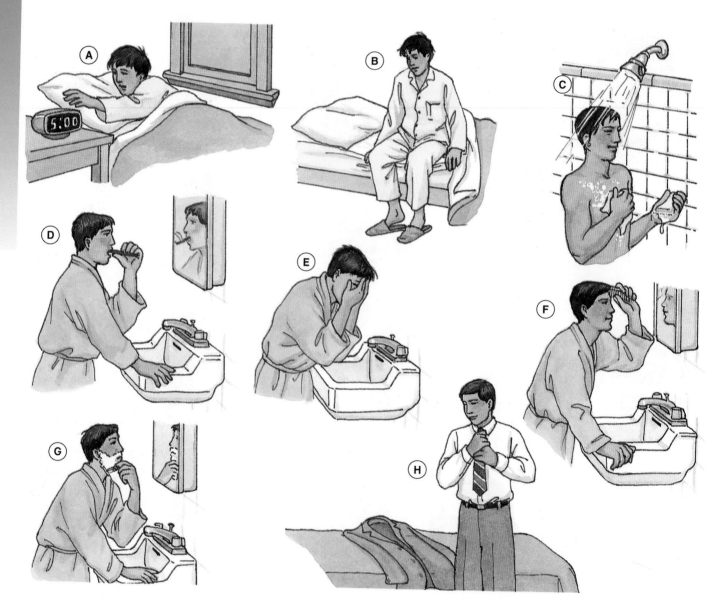

despertarse	**A.** wake up
levantarse	**B.** get up
darse una ducha	**C.** take a shower
cepillarse los dientes	**D.** brush . . . teeth

lavarse la cara	**E.** wash . . . face
peinarse	**F.** comb . . . hair
afeitarse	**G.** shave
vestirse	**H.** get dressed

Language note:

wake up → *wakes up*
get up → *gets up*
brush . . . teeth → *brushes teeth*

Talk about the pictures. Point.

First, he <u>gets up</u>.
Then, he <u>takes a shower</u>.
Next, he <u>brushes his teeth</u>.

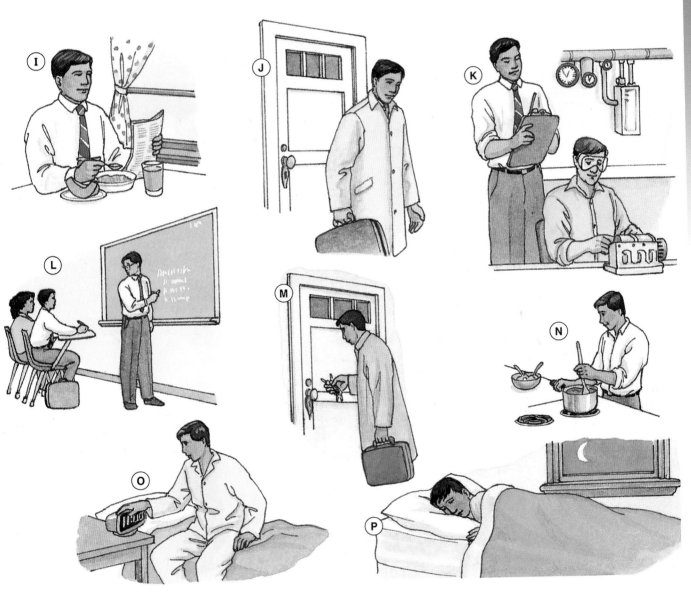

desayunarse	**I.** eat breakfast
salir de casa	**J.** leave the house
trabajar	**K.** work
estudiar / aprender	**L.** study / learn

regresar a casa	**M.** come home
cocinar la cena	**N.** cook dinner
acostarse	**O.** go to bed
dormirse	**P.** go to sleep

Ask and answer questions.
Use pictures I, K, L, N.

A: *Do you <u>eat breakfast</u> every day?*
B: *Yes, I do. / No, I don't.*

Talk about yourself.

First, I <u>get dressed</u>.
Then, I _____.
Next, I _____.

abuelos	**1.** grandparents	esposo	**9.** husband
padre	**2.** father	esposa	**10.** wife
madre	**3.** mother	padres	**11.** parents
hermana	**4.** sister	hijo	**12.** son
hermano	**5.** brother	hija	**13.** daughter
tío	**6.** uncle	sobrina	**14.** niece
tía	**7.** aunt	sobrino	**15.** nephew
primos	**8.** cousins		

Talk about the little boy's family.
Use pictures 1–8.

He has a sister.
He has an uncle.
He has grandparents.

Talk about your family.

I have a son and a daughter.

dar un regalo a	**A.** give a present to
reír	**B.** laugh
besar	**C.** kiss
sonreír	**D.** smile
cantar	**E.** sing
soplar las velitas	**F.** blow out the candles
sacar una fotografía	**G.** take a picture
beber leche	**H.** drink milk
cortar el pastel / bizcocho	**I.** cut the cake
abrir una tarjeta	**J.** open a card

Language note:

give → giving
laugh → laughing
cut → cutting

Talk about the picture. Point.

She's giving a present to the boy.
He's laughing.
He's kissing the baby.

enojado	**1.** angry	
feliz/contento	**2.** happy	
triste	**3.** sad	
nervioso	**4.** nervous	

aburrido	**5.** bored
asustados	**6.** scared
entusiasmados	**7.** excited

Talk about the people. Point.

She's <u>angry</u>.
He's <u>happy</u>.
They're <u>scared</u>.

A: Ask questions.
B: Answer and point.

A: Who's <u>embarrassed</u>?
B: <u>He</u> is.

sorprendida	**8.** surprised	sediento	**12.** thirsty
preocupada	**9.** worried	avergonzado	**13.** embarrassed
cansado	**10.** tired	melancólico/	**14.** homesick
hambriento	**11.** hungry	nostálgico	

A: Tell your partner how to act.
B: Act it out.
A: You're sad.

Talk about your feelings.
I'm nervous today.
I'm tired today.

nacer	**A.** be born	conseguir un trabajo	**D.** get a job
empezar la escuela	**B.** start school	retirarse / jubilarse	**E.** retire
graduarse	**C.** graduate		

Language note:

Today		In the past
be born	→	was born
start	→	started
graduate	→	graduated
get	→	got
fall	→	fell
have	→	had

Talk about the pictures. Point.

She was born in 1990.
He moved.
They got married.

enamorarse	**F.**	fall in love
casarse	**G.**	get married
divorciarse	**H.**	get divorced
tener un bebé	**I.**	have a baby

mudarse	**J.**	move
enfermarse	**K.**	get sick
morir / fallecer	**L.**	die

Talk about your life.

A: When did you <u>start school</u>?
B: In <u>1998</u>.
A: When did you <u>get married</u>?
B: In <u>2000</u>.
A: When did you <u>move to the U.S.</u>?
B: In <u>1998</u>.

chimenea	**1.** chimney	césped	**8.** lawn
techo	**2.** roof	basurero	**9.** garbage can
porche	**3.** porch	asoleadero	**10.** deck
puerta del frente	**4.** front door	patio	**11.** patio
ventana	**5.** window	patio posterior	**12.** backyard
cochera/garaje	**6.** garage	jardín	**13.** garden
entrada de automóvil	**7.** driveway		

Talk about the house at the top.

The house has a porch.
It doesn't have a deck.

Talk about the house at the bottom.

The house has a patio.
It doesn't have a garage.

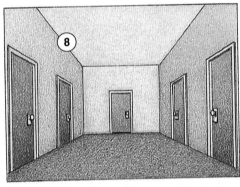

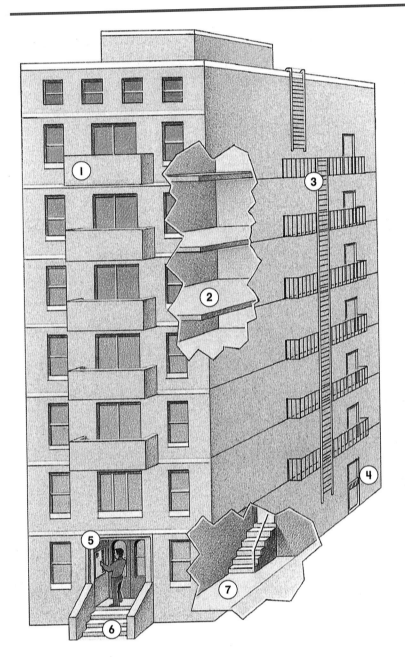

balcón	**1.**	balcony
piso	**2.**	floor
escape de incendio	**3.**	fire escape
salida (de incendio)	**4.**	(fire) exit
entrada	**5.**	entrance
escalones	**6.**	steps
sótano	**7.**	basement

pasillo	**8.**	hall
vestíbulo	**9.**	lobby
ascensor	**10.**	elevator
buzones	**11.**	mailboxes
escalera	**12.**	stairway / stairs
sistema de intercomunicación	**13.**	intercom

Talk about the apartment building.

A: Ask questions.

B: Answer and point.

A: Where's <u>the balcony</u>?

B: Here it is.

A: Where are <u>the steps</u>?

B: Here they are.

Talk about your home.

A: Do you live in an apartment or a house?

B: I live in <u>a house</u>. What about you?

23

techo	**1.** ceiling		mesita	**8.** end table
pared	**2.** wall		mesita central	**9.** coffee table
piso	**3.** floor		alfombra/tapete	**10.** rug
cortinas	**4.** drapes		sofá	**11.** couch/sofa
sillón	**5.** armchair/easy chair		librero/estante	**12.** bookcase
lámpara	**6.** lamp		estéreo	**13.** stereo (system)
teléfono	**7.** (tele)phone		televisión/tele	**14.** television/TV

Talk about the living room. Point.

There's an armchair.
There's a lamp.
There are drapes.

Talk about your living room.

I have a couch in my living room.
I have two rugs, too.

horno microondas	1. microwave (oven)
olla / caldero	2. pot
tetera	3. (tea)kettle
quemador	4. burner
sartén	5. skillet / (frying) pan
estufa / hornillo	6. stove / range
horno	7. oven
asador	8. broiler

abrelatas	9. can opener
fregadero	10. kitchen sink
basurero	11. trash can
gabinete	12. cabinet
tostadora	13. toaster
mostrador	14. counter
congelador	15. freezer
refrigerador / nevera	16. refrigerator

Talk about the kitchen.

A: Ask questions.

B: Answer and point.

A: Where's the microwave?

B: Here it is.

Talk about your kitchen.

I have an oven, a _____, and a _____.

25

clóset	**1.** closet
cómoda/gavetero	**2.** dresser/bureau
cajón/gaveta	**3.** drawer
acondicionador de aire	**4.** air conditioner
cortinas	**5.** curtains
alfombra	**6.** carpet
cama	**7.** bed

almohada	**8.** pillow
funda	**9.** pillowcase
colcha	**10.** bedspread
cobija	**11.** blanket
sábanas	**12.** sheets
reloj despertador	**13.** alarm clock
mesa de noche	**14.** night table

Talk about the bedroom. Point.

There's a closet.
There are curtains.

Name four things you use on a bed.

Talk about your bedroom.

I have an alarm clock and a dresser.
I have two beds.

ducha	**1.** shower
cortina de baño	**2.** shower curtain
llave / grifo	**3.** faucet
desagüe / drenaje	**4.** drain
tina / bañera	**5.** bathtub
basurero	**6.** wastebasket
lavabo	**7.** sink

espejo	**8.** mirror
botiquín	**9.** medicine chest / medicine cabinet
canasta	**10.** hamper
toalla	**11.** towel
inodoro	**12.** toilet
papel higiénico	**13.** toilet paper

Talk about the bathroom. Point.

There's a shower.
There's toilet paper.

A: Ask the question and point.
B: Answer.
A: *What's this?*
B: *A drain.*

hacer la cama	**A.** make the bed	lavar los platos	**F.** wash the dishes
ordenar el cuarto	**B.** pick up/straighten up the room	secar los platos	**G.** dry the dishes
		regar las plantas	**H.** water the plants
limpiar el baño	**C.** clean the bathroom	rastrillar las hojas	**I.** rake the leaves
aspirar la alfombra	**D.** vacuum the rug	sacar la basura	**J.** take out the garbage
sacudir los muebles	**E.** dust the furniture		

Language note:

make → making
pick up → picking up
mop → mopping

Talk about the picture. Point.

She's <u>making the bed</u>.
They're <u>straightening up the room</u>.
He's <u>cleaning the bathroom</u>.

vaciar el basurero	**K.** empty the wastebasket	limpiar / trapear el piso	**O.** mop the floor
cambiar las sábanas	**L.** change the sheets	lavar la ropa	**P.** do the laundry
barrer el piso	**M.** sweep the floor	plantar un árbol	**Q.** plant a tree
lavar las ventanas	**N.** wash the windows	cortar el césped	**R.** mow the lawn

A: Ask questions and point.
B: Answer.
A: *What's he doing?*
B: *He's emptying the wastebasket.*

A: Ask the question. Act it out.
B: Guess.
A: *What am I doing?*
B: *You're mowing the lawn.*

Talk about your housework.
I wash the dishes and do the laundry.

29

limpiador / trapeador	**1.** mop		guantes de hule	**7.** rubber gloves
escoba	**2.** broom		cepillo	**8.** (scrub) brush
recogedor	**3.** dustpan		esponja	**9.** sponge
aspiradora	**4.** vacuum cleaner		toallas de papel	**10.** paper towels
trapo	**5.** cloth / rag		cubeta	**11.** bucket
limpiador	**6.** cleanser		toma de corriente	**12.** outlet

Talk about the picture.

A: Ask questions.

B: Answer and point.

A: *Where's the mop?*

B: *Here it is.*

A: *Where are the paper towels?*

B: *Here they are.*

Talk about yourself.

A: *What do you use to clean?*

B: *I use a sponge and rubber gloves.*

pinzas	**1.** pliers		caja de herramientas	**9.** toolbox
llave de tuerca	**2.** wrench		escalera	**10.** (step)ladder
destornillador	**3.** screwdriver		manguera	**11.** hose
martillo	**4.** hammer		rastrillo	**12.** rake
serrucho	**5.** saw		pala	**13.** shovel
taladro	**6.** drill		cortadora de césped	**14.** lawn mower
cinta de medir	**7.** tape measure		clavo	**15.** nail
linterna eléctrica	**8.** flashlight		tornillo	**16.** screw

Name the tools. Point.

These are pliers.
This is a wrench.

A: Ask the question. Act it out.
B: Guess.

A: *What am I using?*
B: *A rake.*

gotera	**1.** leaking roof / ceiling
pared cuarteada	**2.** cracked wall
ventana rota	**3.** broken window
techo cuarteado	**4.** cracked ceiling

no hay calefacción	**5.** no heat
inodoro tapado	**6.** stopped-up toilet
no hay agua caliente	**7.** no hot water
cerradura rota	**8.** broken lock

Talk about the problems. Point.

There's a leaking roof.
There's no heat.
There are cockroaches.
The refrigerator's not working.

A: Ask the question and point.
B: Answer.

A: What's the problem?
B: There's a cracked wall.

escalones dañados	**9.** broken steps
llave de agua / grifo con gotera	**10.** dripping faucet
desagüe tapado	**11.** clogged drain
refrigerador / nevera descompuesto(a)	**12.** refrigerator not working

cucarachas	**13.** (cock)roaches
ratones	**14.** mice
sótano inundado	**15.** flooded basement

Language note:

a leaking roof	The roof is leaking.
a broken lock	The lock is broken.
a clogged drain	The drain is clogged.

Look at pictures 1–4, 6, 8–11, 15.
Ask and answer questions.

A: *What's wrong with the ceiling?*
B: *It's leaking.*
A: *What's wrong with the steps?*
B: *They're broken.*

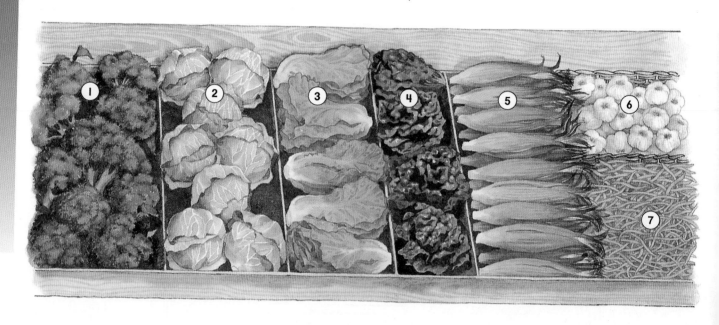

brócoli / brécol	**1.** broccoli	pimiento	**9.** (bell) pepper
col / repollo	**2.** cabbage	pepino	**10.** cucumber
lechuga	**3.** lettuce	papa	**11.** potato
espinaca	**4.** spinach	cebolla	**12.** onion
maíz	**5.** corn	zanahoria	**13.** carrot
ajo	**6.** garlic	hongos	**14.** mushrooms
habichuelas tiernas / ejotes	**7.** string beans	chícharos	**15.** peas
tomate	**8.** tomato		

Name the vegetables. Point.

Here's the broccoli.
Here are the string beans.

Talk about yourself.

What vegetables do you like?
What vegetables don't you like?

plátanos/guineos	**1.** bananas	limones verdes	**8.** limes
uvas	**2.** grapes	ciruelas	**9.** plums
manzanas	**3.** apples	duraznos/	**10.** peaches
naranjas	**4.** oranges	melocotones	
peras	**5.** pears	fresas	**11.** strawberries
toronjas	**6.** grapefruit	cerezas	**12.** cherries
limones	**7.** lemons	sandías	**13.** watermelons
		nueces	**14.** nuts

Name the fruits in the green basket.
Count the fruits in pictures 6, 9–10.

There are _____ grapefruit, _____ plums, and _____ peaches.

Talk about yourself.

A: *Do you like <u>bananas</u>?*
B: *Yes, I do. / No, I don't.*

35

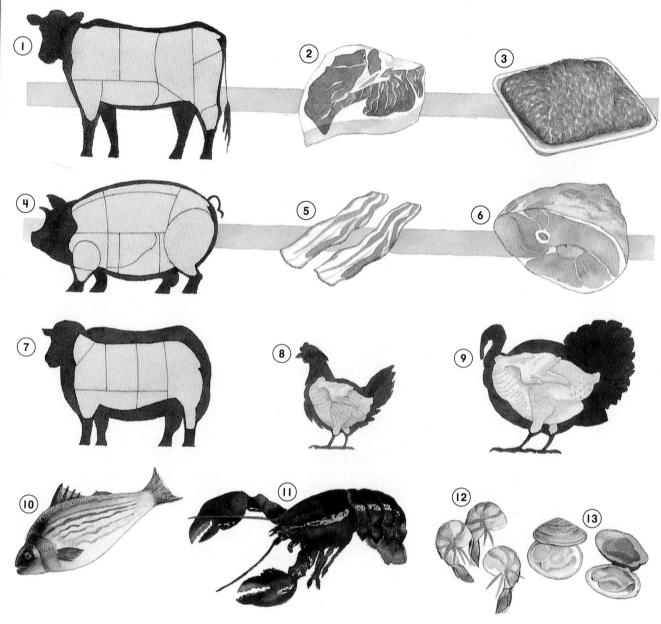

carne de res	**1.** beef	pollo	**8.** chicken
biftec/bistec	**2.** steak	pavo	**9.** turkey
carne molida	**3.** ground meat	pescado	**10.** fish
cerdo/ carne de puerco	**4.** pork	langosta	**11.** lobster
		camarones	**12.** shrimp
tocino	**5.** bacon	almejas	**13.** clams
jamón	**6.** ham		
cordero	**7.** lamb		

Name the meat or seafood. Point.

This is <u>beef</u>.
These are <u>clams</u>.

Talk about yourself.

I eat _____ and _____ .
I don't eat _____ and _____ .

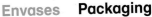

un cartón de leche	**1.** a carton of milk	un frasco de café	**7.** a jar of coffee
un recipiente de yogur	**2.** a container of yogurt	una lata de sopa	**8.** a can of soup
una botella de soda	**3.** a bottle of soda	un rollo de papel higiénico	**9.** a roll of toilet paper
un paquete de galletas	**4.** a package of cookies	una caja de cereal	**10.** a box of cereal
un paquete de pan	**5.** a loaf of bread	una barra de jabón	**11.** a bar of soap
una bolsa de harina	**6.** a bag of flour	un tubo de pasta dental	**12.** a tube of toothpaste

Name the pictures. Point.

This is a carton of milk.

Language note:

1 carton	*2 cartons*
1 loaf	*2 loaves*
1 box	*2 boxes*

Talk about shopping for food.

A: *What do you need from the store?*
B: *A can of soup, two loaves of bread, and two boxes of cereal.*

37

leche	1. milk		yogur	8. yogurt
crema	2. cream		pan	9. bread
azúcar	3. sugar		cereal	10. cereal
huevos	4. eggs		café	11. coffee
queso	5. cheese		té	12. tea
mantequilla	6. butter		harina	13. flour
margarina	7. margarine		aceite	14. oil

Talk about the food.
• Name the things you can drink.
• Name the things you can eat.
• Name the things you can put on food.

Talk about yourself.
A: *What do you like to drink?*
B: <u>*Milk.*</u>
A: *What do you like to eat?*
B: <u>*Cheese.*</u>

arroz	**15.** rice	galletas	**21.** cookies
frijoles/habichuelas	**16.** (dried) beans	sal	**22.** salt
pasta/fideos	**17.** pasta/noodles	pimienta	**23.** pepper
sopa	**18.** soup	mostaza	**24.** mustard
soda/refresco	**19.** soda/pop	salsa de tomate	**25.** ketchup
jugo	**20.** juice	mayonesa	**26.** mayonnaise

Talk about shopping for food.

A: *What can I get you from the store?*

B: *Rice, sugar, and oil*, thanks.

anaquel / estante	**1.** shelf		báscula / balanza	**7.** scale
pasillo	**2.** aisle		caja registradora	**8.** cash register
canasta de compras	**3.** shopping basket		mostrador de pago	**9.** checkout (counter)
carrito de compras	**4.** shopping cart		abarrotes / víveres	**10.** groceries
cliente	**5.** customer		bolsa	**11.** bag
cajera	**6.** checker / checkout person		empacador	**12.** packer / bagger
			regreso de botellas	**13.** bottle return

Name the things in the supermarket. Point.

This is a shelf.
This is an aisle.
These are groceries.

A: Ask questions and point.
B: Answer.

A: *Does he work here?*
B: *Yes, he does. He's a packer.*
    No, he doesn't. He's a customer.

empujar	**A.** push	poner / meter	**E.** put in
llevar / cargar	**B.** carry	sacar	**F.** take out
pagar	**C.** pay for	pesar	**G.** weigh
escoger	**D.** choose / pick out	empacar	**H.** pack

Language note:

push → pushing
put in → putting in
take out → taking out

Talk about the picture. Point.

He's _packing groceries_.
She's _carrying a bag_.

A: Ask the question. Act it out.
B: Guess.
A: _What am I doing?_
B: _You're pushing a shopping cart._

mesa	**1.** table		platillo	**8.** saucer
cubiertos	**2.** silverware		salero y pimentero	**9.** salt and pepper shakers
mantelito individual	**3.** place mat			
tazón/plato hondo	**4.** bowl		servilleta	**10.** napkin
plato	**5.** plate		tenedor	**11.** fork
vaso	**6.** glass		cuchillo	**12.** knife
taza	**7.** cup		cuchara	**13.** spoon

Language note:

1 place mat	2 place mats
1 glass	2 glasses
1 knife	2 knives

silverware = forks, knives, spoons

Talk about the picture.
Ask and answer questions about items 3–13.
A: How many place mats are there?
B: Four.

Talk about yourself.
I use _____, _____, and _____ on my table.

cocinero	**1.** cook	mesera/camarera	**7.** waitress
lavaplatos	**2.** dishwasher	menú	**8.** menu
casilla/caseta	**3.** booth	silla alta	**9.** high chair
agua	**4.** water	sección de fumar	**10.** smoking section
limpiamesas	**5.** busboy	sección de no fumar	**11.** no smoking section
mesero/camarero	**6.** waiter	cajera	**12.** cashier

Talk about the restaurant.

A: Ask questions and point.

B: Answer.

A: *Who's this?*

B: *A cook.*

A: *What's this?*

B: *A booth.*

Breakfast   Lunch   OR

huevos revueltos | **1.** scrambled eggs
salchicha | **2.** sausage
huevos fritos/ estrellados | **3.** fried eggs
pan tostado | **4.** toast
panecillo/ panecillo inglés | **5.** muffin/English muffin
wafles | **6.** waffles

panqueques | **7.** pancakes
jarabe/almíbar | **8.** syrup
donas | **9.** donuts
emparedado | **10.** sandwich
hamburguesa | **11.** hamburger
papas fritas | **12.** french fries
perro caliente | **13.** hot dog

Talk about the food.
• **Name three foods you like to eat for breakfast.**
• **Name three foods you like to eat for lunch.**
• **Name three foods you like to eat for dinner.**

Talk about yourself.
A: *What do you eat for* <u>breakfast</u>?
B: *I eat* <u>scrambled eggs</u> *and* <u>a muffin</u>.

44

Dinner

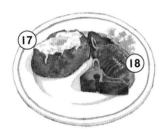

Dessert

ensalada	**14.** salad	puré de papas	**19.** mashed potatoes
espaguetis	**15.** spaghetti	pollo frito	**20.** fried chicken
piza	**16.** pizza	helado	**21.** ice cream
papa al horno	**17.** baked potato	pastel de manzana	**22.** apple pie
chuleta de puerco	**18.** pork chop		

Talk about ordering in a restaurant.

A: *What can I get you?*

B: *I'll have a sandwich, french fries, and ice cream, please.*

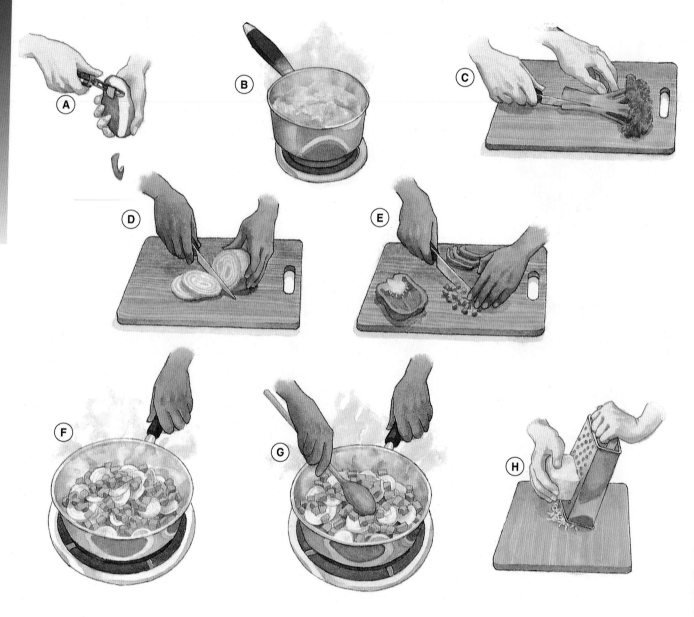

pelar papas	**A.** peel potatoes	picar pimientos	**E.** chop peppers
hervir agua	**B.** boil water	freír cebollas y pimientos	**F.** fry onions and peppers
cortar brócoli/brécol	**C.** cut broccoli	menear cebollas y pimientos	**G.** stir onions and peppers
rebanar cebollas	**D.** slice onions	rallar queso	**H.** grate cheese

Language note:

peel → peeling
cut → cutting
slice → slicing

Talk about the pictures. Point.
She's peeling potatoes.

A: Ask the question. Act it out.
B: Guess.

A: *What am I doing?*
B: *You're chopping something.*

cocer vegetales
al vapor

I. steam vegetables

vaciar leche   **J.** pour milk

mezclar   **K.** mix ingredients
ingredientes

hornear un guiso   **L.** bake a casserole

asar pescado   **M.** broil fish

Use the new words with pages 34–35.
Ask and answer questions.

A: *What foods do you* *steam?*
B: *I* *steam* *carrots.*

Language note:

First, slice onions.
Then, chop peppers.
Next, fry onions and peppers.

Talk about preparing a food you like.

I like to make _____ .
First, *grate cheese.*

vestido	**1.** dress		pantalones	**7.** pants
blusa	**2.** blouse		zapato	**8.** shoe
falda	**3.** skirt		traje	**9.** suit
camisa	**4.** shirt		gorra	**10.** cap
corbata	**5.** tie		uniforme	**11.** uniform
cinturón	**6.** belt			

Talk about the people. Point.

She's wearing <u>a dress</u>.
He's wearing <u>pants</u> and <u>shoes</u>.

Talk about yourself.

I'm wearing _____ and _____.

48

traje de baño (de hombre)	1. swimtrunks/ bathing suit	gorra de béisbol	6. baseball cap
traje de baño (de mujer)	2. swimsuit/bathing suit	camiseta zapatos de tenis	7. T-shirt 8. sneakers/ athletic shoes
anteojos/ gafas de sol	3. sunglasses		9. shorts
jeans	4. jeans	pantalón corto sudadera/traje de entrenamiento	10. warm-up suit
sandalias	5. sandals		

Talk about the people. Point.

He's wearing a bathing suit.
She's wearing jeans and a T-shirt.
They're wearing athletic shoes.

A: **Ask questions and point.**
B: **Answer.**

A: *What are they wearing?*
B: *Shorts and T-shirts.*
A: *What's she wearing?*
B: *Sunglasses and sandals.*

chamarra/chaqueta	**1.** jacket	impermeable	**8.** raincoat
chaleco (de plumón)	**2.** (down) vest	paraguas	**9.** umbrella
suéter	**3.** sweater	bufanda	**10.** scarf
gorra	**4.** hat	abrigo	**11.** coat
sudadera	**5.** sweatshirt	mitones	**12.** mittens
mochila	**6.** backpack	guantes	**13.** gloves
botas	**7.** boots	orejeras	**14.** earmuffs

Talk about the people.
A: Ask questions.
B: Answer and point.
A: *Who's wearing a jacket?*
B: *He is.*

A: *Who's wearing gloves?*
B: *She is.*

Talk about yourself.
A: *What do you wear in cold weather?*
B: *A coat and gloves.*

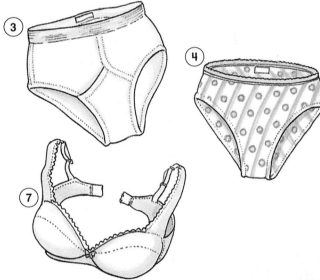

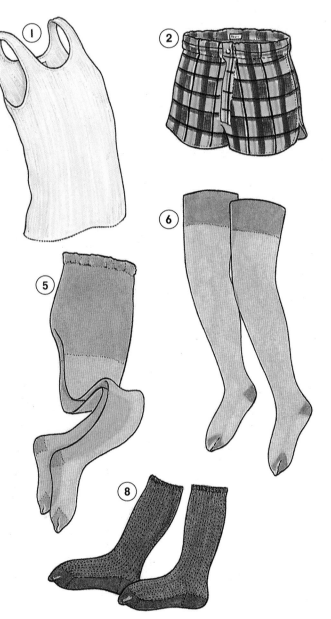

camiseta	**1.** undershirt	sostén	**7.** bra
calzoncillos	**2.** boxer shorts	calcetines	**8.** socks
trusa	**3.** underpants	bata de noche	**9.** nightgown
pantaleta	**4.** panties	pijama	**10.** pajamas
pantimedia	**5.** pantyhose	bata de baño	**11.** bathrobe
medias	**6.** stockings	pantuflas	**12.** slippers

Talk about the clothes.
- **Name the clothes for men.**
- **Name the clothes for women.**
- **Name the clothes for men and women.**

Language note:
a pair of socks
a pair of slippers
Name five things that come in pairs.

51

gruesa	**1.** heavy		sucia	**6.** dirty
ligera	**2.** light		alto	**7.** high
nueva	**3.** new		bajo	**8.** low
vieja	**4.** old		angosta	**9.** narrow
limpia	**5.** clean		ancha	**10.** wide

Language note:

The opposite of **heavy** is **light**.
The opposite of **narrow** is **wide**.

Look at pictures 1–16.
Ask and answer questions.

A: *What's the opposite of new?*
B: *Old.*

mojado	**11.** wet	suelta	**16.** loose
seco	**12.** dry	pequeña	**17.** small
larga	**13.** long	mediana	**18.** medium
corta	**14.** short	grande	**19.** large
apretada	**15.** tight	extra grande	**20.** extra-large

Talk about pictures 11–16. Point.

Her hair is <u>wet</u>.
Her skirt is <u>long</u>.
His shirt is <u>tight</u>.

A: Ask questions about 17–20 and point.
B: Answer.
A: What size is that shirt?
B: It's <u>a small</u>. / It's <u>an extra-large</u>.

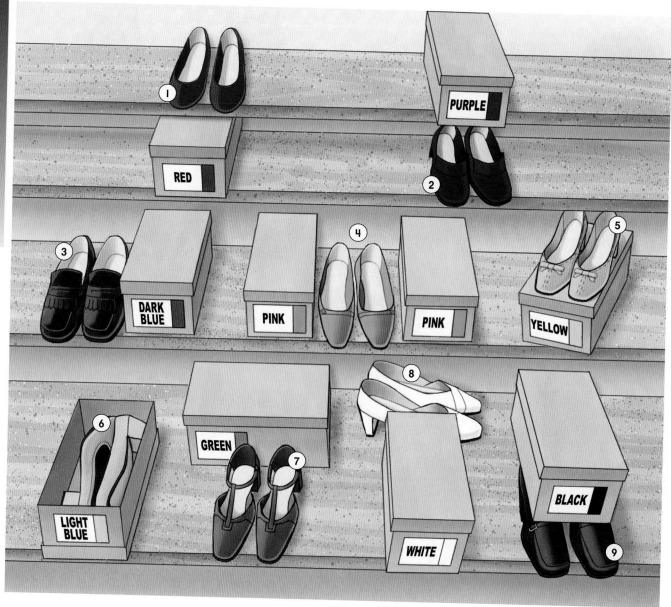

por encima de la caja	**1.** above the box	dentro de la caja	**6.** in the box
por debajo de la caja	**2.** below the box	frente a la caja	**7.** in front of the box
junto a la caja	**3.** next to the box	detrás de la caja	**8.** behind the box
entre las cajas	**4.** between the boxes	debajo de la caja	**9.** under the box
sobre la caja	**5.** on the box		

Talk about the shoes. Point.

The red shoes are above the box.
The white shoes are behind the box.

Ask and answer questions.

A: *Where are the yellow shoes?*
B: *On the box.*

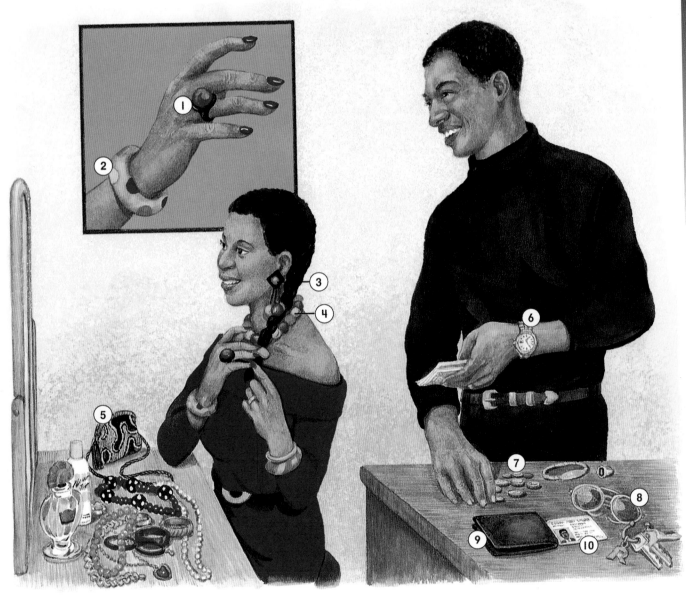

anillo	**1.** ring		reloj	**6.** watch
pulsera	**2.** bracelet		cambio	**7.** change
aretes	**3.** earrings		lentes/anteojos/	**8.** glasses
collar	**4.** necklace		gafas	
bolsa	**5.** purse/bag		cartera/billetera	**9.** wallet
			tarjeta	**10.** ID card
			de identificación	

Talk about the picture. Count.

She has _____ necklaces and _____ bracelets.
She's wearing _____ necklace and
_____ bracelets.

Language note:

I carry a wallet / change / an ID card.
I wear earrings / a ring.

Ask and answer questions.

A: What do you carry with you?
B: A wallet.
A: What do you usually wear?
B: Earrings.

Talk about yourself.

I'm wearing _____.

lavadora	**1.** washer / washing machine
detergente	**2.** detergent
secadora	**3.** dryer
ranura	**4.** slot
canasta de lavandería	**5.** laundry basket
tabla de planchar	**6.** ironing board
plancha	**7.** iron

poner / meter	**A.** load / put in
sacar	**B.** unload / take out
planchar	**C.** iron
doblar	**D.** fold

Talk about pictures 1–7.
Here's the washing machine.

A: **Tell your partner what to do.**
B: **Act it out.**

A: *Load the washing machine.*
Take out the clothes.

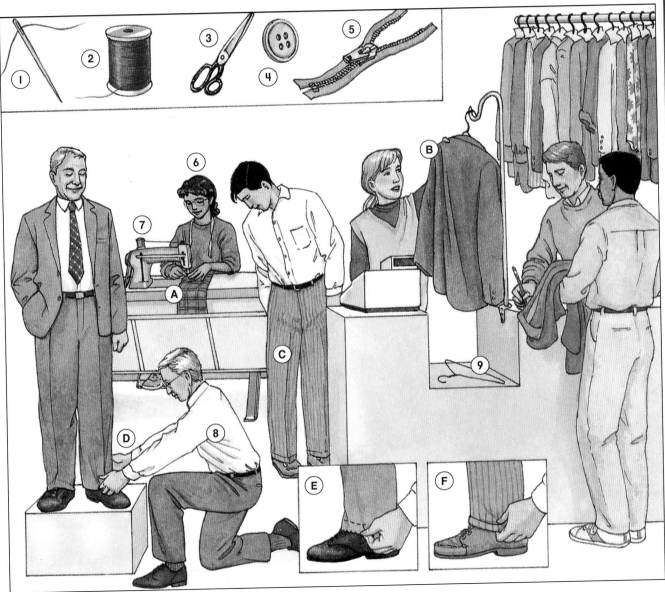

aguja	**1.** needle	coser	**A.** sew
hilo	**2.** thread	colgar	**B.** hang up
tijeras	**3.** scissors	probarse	**C.** try on
botón	**4.** button	corregir/	**D.** alter/do alterations
cierre	**5.** zipper	hacer arreglos	
costurera	**6.** seamstress	alargar	**E.** lengthen
máquina de coser	**7.** sewing machine	acortar	**F.** shorten
sastre	**8.** tailor		
gancho	**9.** hanger		

Look at pictures 1–9.
- **Name four things for sewing.**
- **Name two people who sew.**

Look at pictures A–F.
A: **Tell your partner what to do.**
B: **Act it out.**

A: *Please <u>sew</u> this jacket.*
Please <u>hang up</u> this jacket.

cara	**1.** face		dedo	**8.** finger
cuello	**2.** neck		pulgar	**9.** thumb
hombro	**3.** shoulder		muñeca	**10.** wrist
pecho	**4.** chest		cabeza	**11.** head
mano	**5.** hand		brazo	**12.** arm
cintura	**6.** waist		seno	**13.** breast
cadera	**7.** hip		pierna	**14.** leg

Talk about the pictures.

A: Ask the question and point.

B: Answer.

A: *What's this?*

B: *His face. / Her back.*

espalda	**15.** back		talón	**22.** heel
muslo	**16.** thigh		dedo del pie	**23.** toe
codo	**17.** elbow		cerebro	**24.** brain
rodilla	**18.** knee		pulmón	**25.** lung
pantorrilla	**19.** calf		corazón	**26.** heart
tobillo	**20.** ankle		estómago	**27.** stomach
pie	**21.** foot			

**A: Tell your partner what to do.
Use words 15–23.**

B: Act it out.

A: Point to your <u>elbow</u>.

**Use the new words with pages 48–49.
Talk about the people. Point.**

This is <u>his knee</u>.
This is <u>her shoulder</u>.

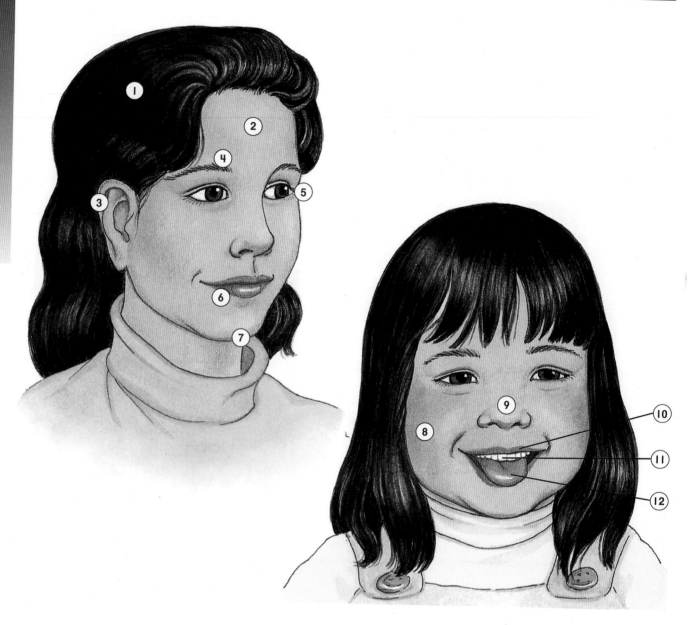

cabello/pelo	**1.** hair		mentón	**7.** chin
frente	**2.** forehead		mejilla	**8.** cheek
oreja	**3.** ear		nariz	**9.** nose
ceja	**4.** eyebrow		labio	**10.** lip
ojo	**5.** eye		diente	**11.** tooth
boca	**6.** mouth		lengua	**12.** tongue

Talk about the pictures.

A: Ask the question and point.

B: Answer.

A: *What's this?*

B: *Her <u>hair</u>.*

Use the new words with page 24.
Talk about the woman. Point.

This is her <u>forehead</u>.

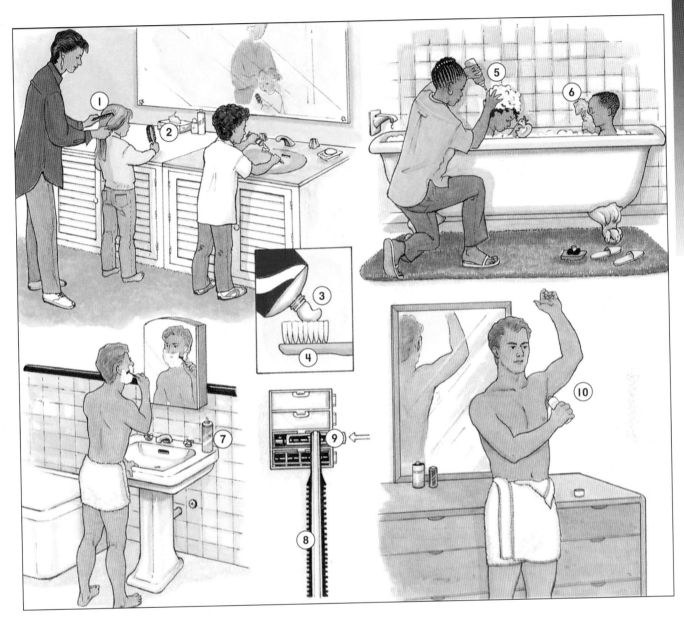

peine	1. comb
cepillo	2. brush
pasta de dientes	3. toothpaste
cepillo de dientes	4. toothbrush
champú	5. shampoo
paño para lavarse	6. washcloth
crema de afeitar	7. shaving cream
navaja de afeitar	8. razor
hojas de afeitar	9. blades
desodorante	10. deodorant

Talk about the pictures. Point.

She's using a comb.
He's using shaving cream.

A: **Ask the question. Act it out.**
B: **Guess.**

A: *What am I using?*
B: *Toothpaste and a toothbrush.*

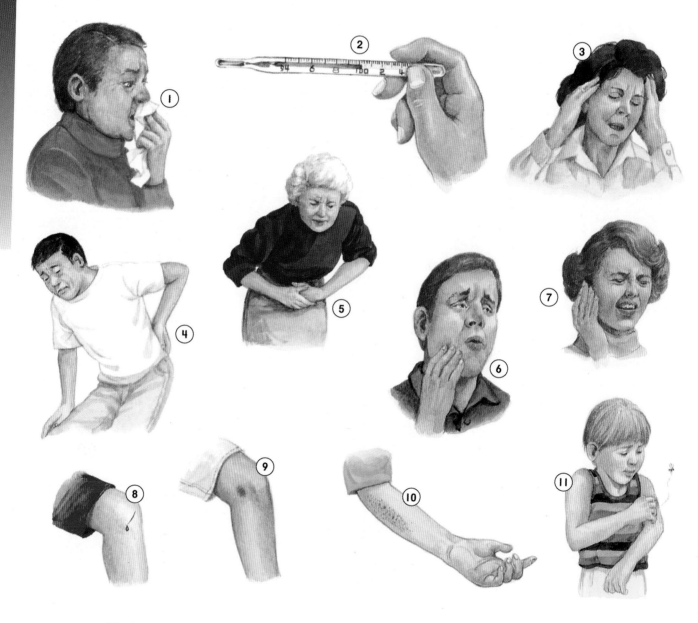

resfriado	**1.** cold
fiebre	**2.** fever
dolor de cabeza	**3.** headache
dolor de espalda	**4.** backache
dolor de estómago	**5.** stomachache
dolor de diente/ muela	**6.** toothache
dolor de oído	**7.** earache
cortadura	**8.** cut
contusión	**9.** bruise
sarpullido	**10.** rash
picadura de insecto	**11.** insect bite

Talk about pictures 1–17. Point.

He has <u>a cold</u>.
She has <u>an earache</u>.
He has <u>high blood pressure</u>.

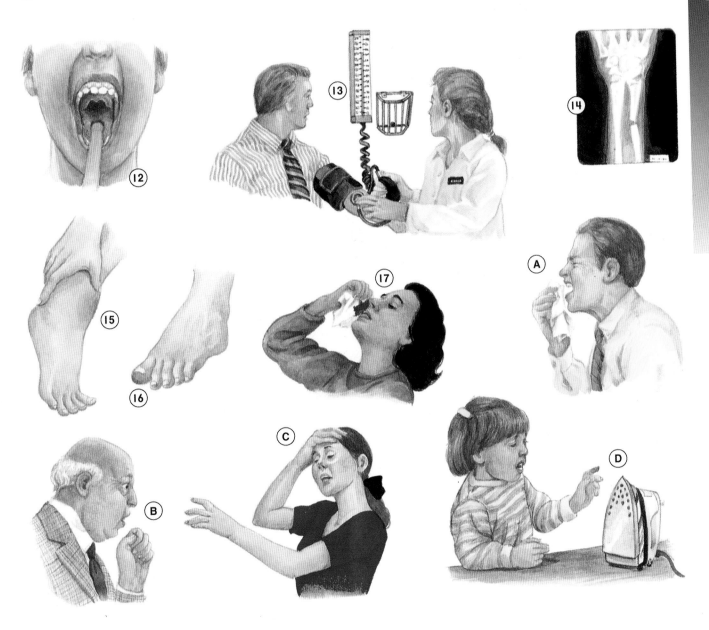

dolor de garganta	**12.**	sore throat
alta presión	**13.**	high blood pressure
brazo roto	**14.**	broken arm
tobillo hinchado	**15.**	swollen ankle
dedo del pie infectado	**16.**	infected toe
nariz sangrienta	**17.**	bloody nose

estornudar	**A.**	sneeze
toser	**B.**	cough
desmayarse	**C.**	faint
quemarse	**D.**	burn . . . self

A: Ask the question and point.
B: Answer.

A: *What's the matter?*
B: *She has a headache.*

Talk about pictures A–C.

He's going to sneeze.

tener una operación	**A.** have an operation
descansar	**B.** get rest
tener puntos	**C.** get stitches
tomar medicina	**D.** take medicine
ser enyesado	**E.** get a cast
hacer ejercicio	**F.** exercise
ponerse a dieta	**G.** diet

medicinas/drogas	**1.** medicine/drugs
píldoras	**2.** pills
crema/ungüento	**3.** cream/ointment
inyección	**4.** injection/shot
gotas	**5.** drops
gotero	**6.** medicine dropper
atomizador	**7.** spray

Language note:

have → having
get → getting

Talk about pictures A–G. Point.

She's *having an operation*.
He's *getting rest*.

A: Ask questions about 1–7.
B: Answer and point.

A: Where are *the pills*?
B: Here they are.
A: Where's *the cream*?
B: Here it is.

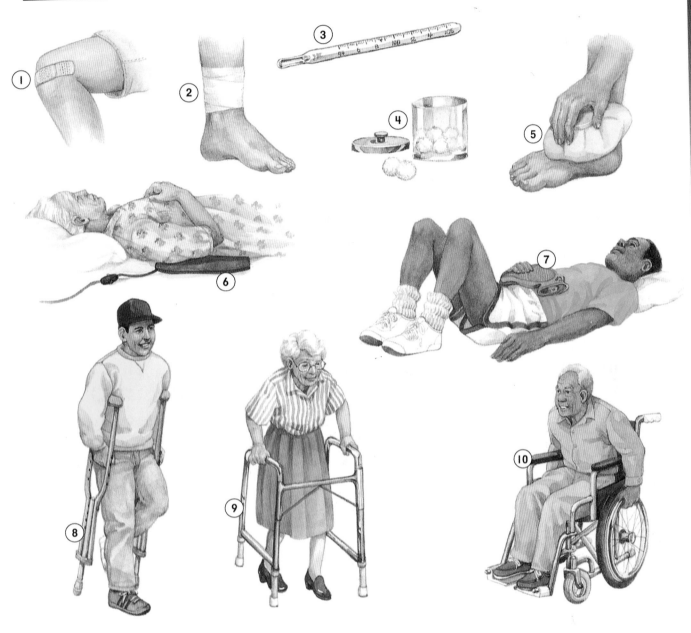

curita	1. Band-Aid	toalla calentadora	6. heating pad
vendaje	2. bandage	bolsa de agua caliente	7. hot water bottle
termómetro	3. thermometer		
bolitas de algodón	4. cotton balls	muletas	8. crutches
compresa de hielo	5. ice pack	andador	9. walker
		silla de ruedas	10. wheelchair

Name the items. Point.

This is a Band-Aid.
This is an ice pack.
These are cotton balls.

Use the new words with pages 62–63.
Talk about the people. Point.

He needs a heating pad.
She needs a Band-Aid.

Sara Vanesky

Sara Vanesky

sala de espera	**1.** waiting room	médico	**6.** doctor
recepcionista	**2.** receptionist	enfermera	**7.** nurse
formulario de seguro	**3.** insurance form	sala de reconocimiento	**8.** examining room
tarjeta de seguro	**4.** insurance card	rayos equis	**9.** X ray
paciente	**5.** patient	receta	**10.** prescription

Talk about the pictures. Count.

There are _____ patients in the waiting room.
There are _____ medical workers.

Look at pictures 1–10.

A: Ask questions and point.
B: Answer.

A: *Who's she?*
B: *The receptionist.*
A: *What's this?*
B: *An X ray.*

llenar el formulario	**A.** fill out the form	examinar al paciente	**F.** examine the patient
escribir el nombre en letra de molde	**B.** print name	pesar al paciente	**G.** weigh the patient
firmar el nombre	**C.** sign name	tomar la temperatura	**H.** take . . . temperature
demostrar la tarjeta de seguro	**D.** show insurance card	poner una inyección	**I.** give a shot / an injection
esperar	**E.** wait	escribir una receta	**J.** write a prescription

Talk about the patient in pictures A–D.

First, she <u>fills out the form</u>.

Then, she _____ .

Next, she _____ .

Look at pictures F–J.
Ask and answer questions.

A: What does the doctor do?
B: She <u>examines the patient</u>.
A: What does the nurse do?
B: She <u>takes his temperature</u>.

escuela	**1.**	school
estación de bomberos	**2.**	firehouse
palacio de justicia	**3.**	courthouse
oficina de correos	**4.**	post office
estación de policía/ comisaría	**5.**	police station

iglesia	**6.**	church
parque	**7.**	park
librería	**8.**	bookstore
florería	**9.**	florist
panadería	**10.**	bakery
supermercado	**11.**	supermarket

Talk about the picture. Point.

This is <u>the school</u>.

Language note:

*The bookstore is **next to** the florist.*
*The city hall is **across from** the park.*
*The school is **near** the post office.*

Ask and answer the questions.

A: *Where's <u>the parking garage</u>?*
B: *It's <u>near</u> <u>the park</u>.*
A: *Where's <u>the post office</u>?*
B: *It's <u>next to</u> <u>the police station</u>.*

68

ayuntamiento	**12.** city hall	edificio de oficinas	**17.** office building
estación de autobuses	**13.** bus station	cine	**18.** movie theater
		galería	**19.** mall
estación de trenes	**14.** train station	tienda por departamentos	**20.** department store
estacionamiento	**15.** parking garage		
Departamento de Registro de Vehículos	**16.** Department of Motor Vehicles (DMV)	estacionamiento/ aparcamiento	**21.** parking lot

Ask and answer questions about your community.

A: Is there _a mall_ nearby?
B: Yes, there is.
A: Is there _a train station_?
B: No, there isn't.

Talk about your community.
Name five places you go.

_I go to_ _____, _____, _____, _____,
and _____.

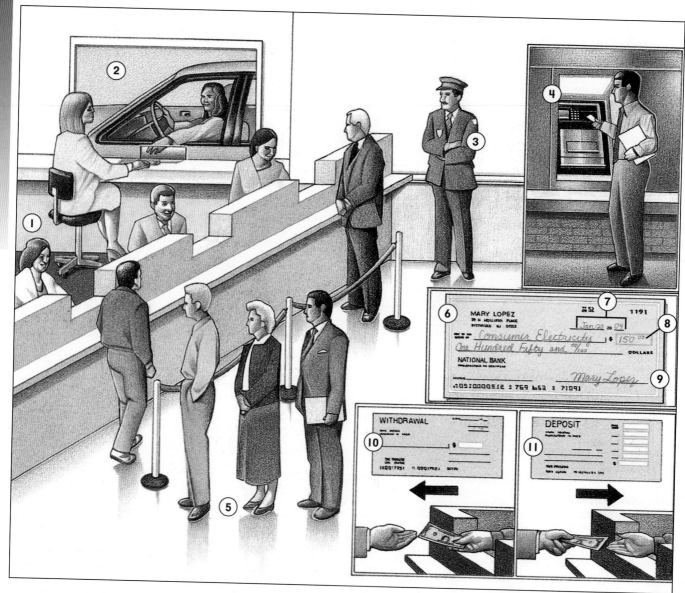

pagadora	1. teller	fecha	7. date
ventana de servicio rápido	2. drive-thru window	cantidad	8. amount
guardia de seguridad	3. security guard	firma	9. signature
pagador automático	4. ATM/cash machine	comprobante de retiro	10. withdrawal slip
cola	5. line	comprobante de depósito	11. deposit slip
cheque	6. check		

Talk about pictures 1–6, 10, 11. Point.
She's a teller.
This is a drive-thru window.
Name three things you can write on a check.

Talk about yourself.
A: *Do you use an ATM?*
B: *Yes, I do. / No, I don't.*
A: *Do you write checks?*
B: *Yes, I do. / No, I don't.*

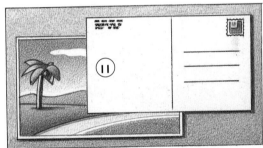

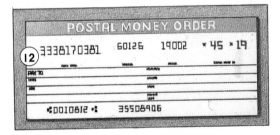

empleado postal	1. postal worker / postal clerk	dirección del remitente	7. return address
paquete	2. package	estampilla / sello postal	8. stamp
cartero	3. letter carrier	dirección	9. address
buzón	4. mailbox	código postal	10. zip code
carta	5. letter	tarjeta postal	11. postcard
sobre	6. envelope	giro postal	12. money order

Talk about pictures 1–6, 11, 12. Point.

He's a postal clerk.
This is a package.

Talk about an envelope.
Use words 7–10. Point.

Put the return address here.

semáforo	**1.** traffic light		puesto de periódicos	**7.** newsstand
peatón	**2.** pedestrian		parquímetro	**8.** parking meter
cruce de peatones	**3.** crosswalk		acera	**9.** sidewalk
teléfono público	**4.** public telephone		borde	**10.** curb
esquina	**5.** corner		parada de autobús	**11.** bus stop
intersección	**6.** intersection		banca	**12.** bench

Talk about the picture. Count.

There are _____ traffic lights.
There are _____ pedestrians.
There are _____ people at the bus stop.

A: Ask questions.
B: Answer and point.

A: *Where's the newsstand?*
B: *Here it is.*
A: *Where are the parking meters?*
B: *Here they are.*

salir de la tienda	**A.** come out of the store
entrar a la tienda	**B.** go into the store
hacer una llamada telefónica	**C.** make a phone call
detenerse	**D.** stop
cruzar la calle	**E.** cross the street
enviar una carta	**F.** mail a letter

comprar víveres	**G.** buy groceries
mirar los escaparates/la ropa	**H.** look at the windows/clothes
caminar	**I.** walk
dar vuelta	**J.** turn
esperar el autobús	**K.** wait for the bus

Language note:

come → coming
stop → stopping
walk → walking

Talk about the picture. Point.

She's coming out of the store.
The bus is stopping.

A: Ask questions.
B: Answer and point.

A: *Who's crossing the street?*
B: *He is.*
A: *Who's mailing a letter?*
B: *She is.*

73

humo	**1.** smoke		policía	**8.** police officer
fuego	**2.** fire		asalto/robo con	**9.** mugging
bombero	**3.** fire fighter		violencia	
accidente	**4.** accident		inundación	**10.** flood
ambulancia	**5.** ambulance		temblor/terremoto	**11.** earthquake
paramédico	**6.** paramedic		tornado	**12.** tornado
robo	**7.** robbery/theft		huracán	**13.** hurricane

Talk about the pictures.
- **Count the emergency workers.**
- **Name them.**

A: **Ask questions about the pictures. Point.**
B: **Answer.**
A: *What happened?*
B: *There was <u>a fire</u>.*
   There was <u>an earthquake</u>.

caerse	**A.** fall (down)	envenenarse	**D.** swallow poison
tener un ataque al corazón	**B.** have a heart attack	sofocarse	**E.** choke
ahogarse	**C.** drown		

Language note:

fall	→	falling
have	→	having
drown	→	drowning

A: Ask questions about pictures A–E. Point.
B: Answer.
A: What's the emergency?
B: She's falling.

Transportation   Transporte

automóvil	**1.** car	tren subterráneo	**7.** subway
autobús	**2.** bus	avión	**8.** plane
camión	**3.** truck	tren	**9.** train
camioneta	**4.** van	barco	**10.** ship
motocicleta	**5.** motorcycle	bicicleta	**11.** bicycle
taxi	**6.** taxi(cab)/cab		

Talk about the pictures.

A: Ask the question and point.

B: Answer.

A: *What's this?*

B: *A car.*

Talk about yourself.

A: *How do you get to school?*

B: *By bus.*

A: *How do you like to travel?*

B: *By train.*

placa / chapa de matrícula	1. license plate	tablero	9. dashboard
faros delanteros	2. headlights	volante	10. steering wheel
batería	3. battery	encendido	11. ignition
capó	4. hood	freno	12. brake
parabrisas	5. windshield	acelerador	13. accelerator / gas pedal
maletera / baúl	6. trunk	cinturón de seguridad	14. seat belt
tanque de gasolina	7. gas tank	asiento para niño	15. car seat
llanta	8. tire		

Talk about the car.
- **Name three things inside the car.**
- **Name three things on the outside of the car.**
- **Name three things the driver uses.**

Ask and answer questions.

A: *Where's the license plate?*
B: *Here it is.*
A: *Where are the headlights?*
B: *Here they are.*

On the Road (Prepositions II)   En la carretera (Preposiciones II)

| sobre la carretera | **1.** over the highway | fuera de la ciudad | **3.** away from the city |
| a/hacia la ciudad | **2.** to/toward the city | a través del túnel | **4.** through the tunnel |

Talk about the picture. Point.

The gray car is going over the highway.
The blue car is going away from the city.

Ask and answer questions.

A: Is the red car going toward the city?
B: Yes, it is. / No, it isn't.

bajando la colina	**5.** down the hill
subiendo la colina	**6.** up the hill
cruzando el tráfico	**7.** across the traffic

entrando a la gasolinera	**8.** into the gas station
saliendo de la gasolinera	**9.** out of the gas station
alrededor del accidente	**10.** around the accident

Ask and answer questions.

A: *Where's the purple car going?*

B: *Up the hill.*

Ask and answer questions. Use pictures 2, 3, 5, 6, 8, 9.

A: *Is the green car going up the hill or down the hill?*

B: *Down the hill.*

pasajero	1. passenger	puerta/salida	6. gate
boleto	2. ticket	auxiliar de vuelo	7. flight attendant
maleta/equipaje	3. suitcase/luggage	piloto	8. pilot
control de seguridad	4. security check	reclamo de equipaje	9. baggage claim
tarjeta de embarque/ pasabordo	5. boarding pass		

Talk about the pictures. Count.

There are _____ passengers.

There are _____ tickets.

There are _____ suitcases.

A: Ask questions about 4–9.

B: Answer and point.

A: *Where's the security check?*

B: *Here it is.*

A: *Where's the flight attendant?*

B: *Here she is.*

facturar equipaje	**A.** check bags	recibir	**E.** meet
salir / partir	**B.** leave / depart	estrecharse las	**F.** shake hands
decir (adiós)	**C.** wave (good-bye)	manos / saludarse	
con la mano		abrazarse	**G.** hug
llegar	**D.** arrive		

Language note:

check → checking
leave → leaving
hug → hugging

Talk about A–G. Point.

He's checking bags.
They're leaving.

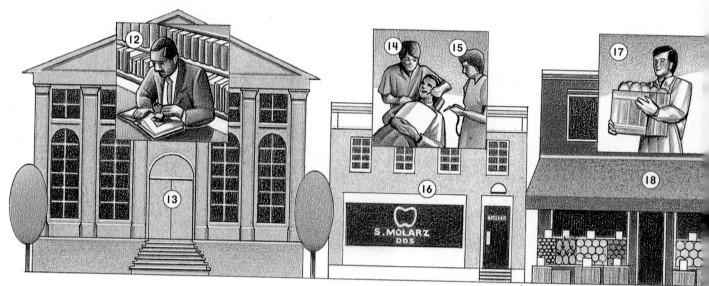

farmacéutico	**1.** pharmacist/druggist	carnicero	**6.** butcher
farmacia	**2.** drugstore	carnicería	**7.** butcher shop
mecánico	**3.** mechanic	estilista/peluquera	**8.** hairdresser/hairstylist
asistente	**4.** attendant	salón de belleza	**9.** beauty salon
gasolinera	**5.** service station/ gas station	barbero/peluquero	**10.** barber
		barbería/peluquería	**11.** barbershop

Talk about the pictures.
- **Name the people who work outdoors.**
- **Name the people who work indoors.**
- **Name the people who work indoors and outdoors.**

Talk about the pictures. Point.

She's a pharmacist. She works in a drugstore.
He's a mechanic. He works in a service station.

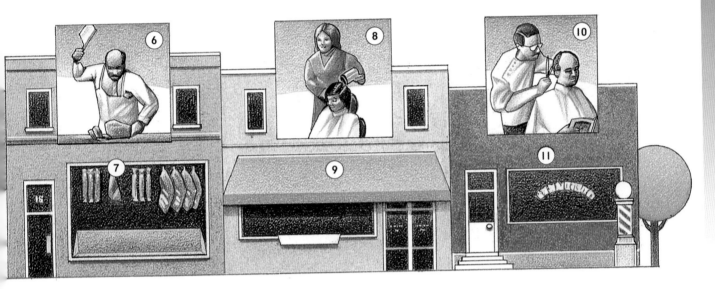

bibliotecario	**12.** librarian	abacero／abarrotero	**17.** grocer
biblioteca	**13.** library	mercado de frutas	**18.** fruit and vegetable
dentista	**14.** dentist	y verduras	market
asistente dental	**15.** dental assistant	trabajador	**19.** sanitation worker
consultorio	**16.** office	de limpieza pública	
		repartidor	**20.** delivery person

Look at pictures 1–18.
Ask and answer questions.

A: *Where does a dentist work?*
B: *In an office.*

Talk about yourself.

A: *Would you like to be a barber?*
B: *Yes, I would. / No, I wouldn't.*

84

plomera	**1.** plumber	conserje	**8.** janitor / custodian
electricista	**2.** electrician	empleado	**9.** mover
cerrajero	**3.** locksmith	de mudanzas	
empleada doméstica	**4.** housekeeper	superintendente	**10.** superintendent / apartment manager
jardinero	**5.** gardener		
pintor	**6.** painter	portero	**11.** doorman
trabajador de construcción	**7.** construction worker	taxista	**12.** taxi driver

Talk about the pictures.
- **Name the workers who wear a uniform.**
- **Name the workers who work outdoors.**
- **Name the workers who work indoors.**
- **Name the workers who drive at work.**

obrero de fábrica	**13.** factory worker
capataz	**14.** foreman
chofer / conductor de autobús	**15.** bus driver
carpintero	**16.** carpenter
empleado de mantenimiento	**17.** maintenance man

pescador	**18.** fisherman
camionero	**19.** truck driver
granjero	**20.** farmer
soldado	**21.** soldier
operaria de máquina de coser	**22.** sewing machine operator
operador de tren	**23.** (train) conductor

A: Ask questions and point.
B: Answer.

A: *What does he do?*
B: *He's a factory worker.*

Talk about yourself.

A: *Would you like to be an electrician?*
B: *Yes, I would. / No, I wouldn't.*

secretaria	1. secretary	contadora	9. accountant
mecanógrafo	2. typist / word processor	abogado	10. lawyer
archivista	3. file clerk	vendedor	11. salesperson
programadora	4. computer programmer	niñera	12. babysitter
mensajero	5. messenger	bailarina / bailarín	13. dancer
fotógrafo	6. photographer	cantante	14. singer
reportera	7. reporter	actor / actriz	15. actor / actress
hombre / mujer de negocios	8. businessman / businesswoman	artista	16. artist

Talk about the pictures.
- **Count the office workers.**
- **Name them.**

A: Ask questions and point.
B: Answer.

A: *What does she do?*
B: *She's a singer.* / *She's an actress.*

quitar	**A.** take out		medir	**G.** measure
poner / colocar	**B.** put in		martillar	**H.** hammer
excavar	**C.** dig		subir	**I.** climb
dirigir / supervisar	**D.** oversee		raspar	**J.** scrape
colocar	**E.** lay		pintar	**K.** paint
vaciar	**F.** pour			

Language note:

take out / put in a window
dig a hole
oversee the work
lay bricks
pour cement

Look at the pictures.
A: **Tell your partner what to do.**
B: **Act it out.**

A: *Take out a window.*
   Measure something.

87

arreglar / reparar teles / aparatos domésticos	**A.** fix / repair TVs / appliances	cortar césped	**F.** cut grass
arreglar / reparar automóviles	**B.** fix / repair cars	vender ropa	**G.** sell clothes
arreglar / reparar plomería	**C.** fix / repair pipes	vender verduras	**H.** sell vegetables
cortar pelo	**D.** cut hair	vender periódicos	**I.** sell newspapers
cortar carne	**E.** cut meat	construir casas	**J.** build houses
		construir muebles	**K.** build furniture

Talk about the pictures.

• **Name three things you can fix.**
• **Name three things you can cut.**
• **Name three things you can sell.**

• **Name three things you can drive.**
• **Name three things you can deliver.**

cuidar a niños	**L.**	take care of children
mantener piscinas	**M.**	take care of pools
cuidar jardines	**N.**	take care of grounds
conducir / manejar un autobús	**O.**	drive a bus
manejar un taxi	**P.**	drive a cab
manejar un camión	**Q.**	drive a truck
repartir correo	**R.**	deliver mail
repartir víveres	**S.**	deliver groceries
repartir paquetes	**T.**	deliver packages
recoger basura	**U.**	collect garbage
cobrar pasajes	**V.**	collect fares
recoger boletos	**W.**	collect tickets

Language note:

He fixes cars.
She sells clothes.
She takes care of children.

A: Ask questions and point.
B: Answer.

A: What does he do?
B: He takes care of pools.

trabajadora de guardería infantil	**1.** day-care worker / child-care worker		juguete	**7.** toy
carrito de bebé	**2.** stroller		babero	**8.** bib
chupón	**3.** pacifier		corralito	**9.** playpen
biberón	**4.** bottle		cuna	**10.** crib
tetilla/pezón	**5.** nipple		sonajero	**11.** rattle
pañal	**6.** diaper		cuna	**12.** cradle

Talk about the picture. Count.

There are _____ day-care workers.

Name three things for babies.

90

traer / dejar	**A.** bring / drop off	tomar una siesta	**G.** take a nap
cambiar pañales	**B.** change diapers	mecer	**H.** rock
jugar	**C.** play	tomar en los brazos	**I.** hold
gatear	**D.** crawl	llorar	**J.** cry
correr	**E.** run	recoger / levantar	**K.** pick up
alimentar	**F.** feed	vestir	**L.** dress

Language note:

drop off → dropping off
change → changing
cry → crying

A: Ask questions.
B: Answer and point.

A: Who's <u>crying</u>?
B: <u>She</u> is.
A: Who's <u>feeding</u> the baby?
B: <u>He</u> is.

Actividades al aire libre	Outdoor Activities
acampar / ir de campamento	**A.** go camping
hacer excursión	**B.** go hiking

Deportes	Sports
jugar tenis	**C.** play tennis
jugar fútbol americano	**D.** play football
jugar baloncesto	**E.** play basketball
jugar fútbol	**F.** play soccer
jugar béisbol	**G.** play baseball
ir a esquiar	**H.** go skiing

Talk about the pictures.
- **Name activities you can do outdoors.**
- **Name activities you can do indoors.**

Talk about yourself.
A: What sports do you play?
B: I play baseball. / I don't play any sports.

Actividades bajo techo	Indoor Activities	Ejercicio	Exercise
tocar un instrumento	**I.** play an instrument	ir a nadar	**M.** go swimming
ir al cine	**J.** go to the movies	ir a correr	**N.** go running
ver televisión	**K.** watch TV		
escuchar música	**L.** listen to music		

Talk about yourself.

A: *What do you like to do?*

B: *I like to <u>listen to music</u>.*

La Nochevieja
beber champaña
brindar

New Year's Eve
A. drink champagne
B. make a toast

El Día de los Enamorados
dar regalos de San Valentín
recibir flores

Valentine's Day

C. give valentines

D. get flowers

La Pascua
pintar huevos de Pascua
ir en busca de huevos de Pascua

Easter
E. paint Easter eggs

F. go on an Easter egg hunt

El Día de los Soldados Muertos
flotar una bandera
ver un desfile
visitar un cementerio

Memorial Day

G. wave a flag
H. watch a parade
I. visit a cemetery

Name the holidays. Point.
New Year's Eve
the Fourth of July

Ask and answer questions.
A: *When do you make a toast?*
B: *On New Year's Eve.*

94

El 4 de julio
hacer una parrillada/
comer al aire libre
ver fuegos artificiales

Fourth of July
J. have a barbecue/
picnic
K. watch fireworks

El Día de las Brujas
esculpir
una calabaza
disfrazarse
salir por obsequios
o travesuras

Halloween
L. carve out a pumpkin

M. wear a costume
N. go trick-or-treating

**El Día de Acción
de Gracias**
reunirse con familia
y amigos
dar gracias
comer una gran
comida

Thanksgiving

O. get together with
family and friends
P. give thanks
Q. eat a big meal

La Navidad
enviar tarjetas
ir de compras
navideñas
decorar el árbol

Christmas
R. send cards
S. go Christmas
shopping
T. decorate the tree

Talk about yourself.

When do you get together with family and friends?
When do you send cards?

95

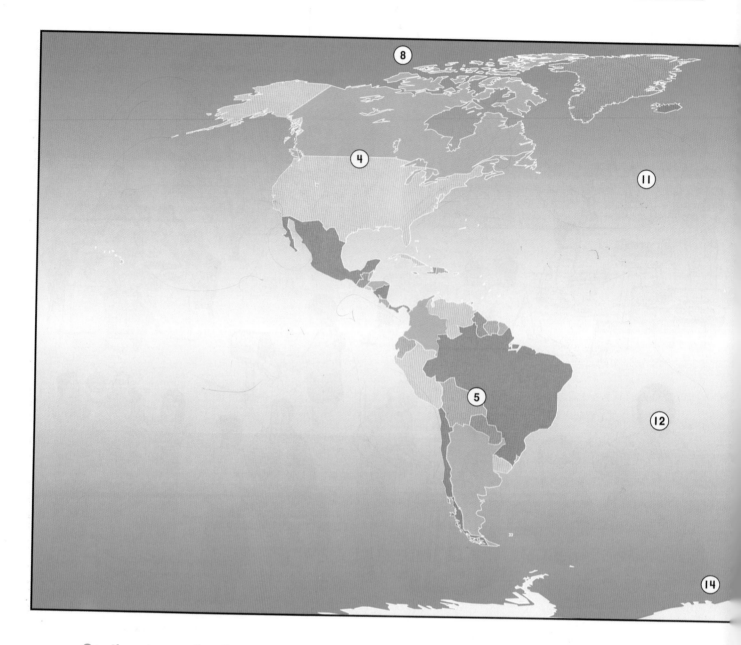

Continentes	**Continents**	Océanos	**Oceans**
Asia	**1.** Asia	Artico	**8.** Arctic
África	**2.** Africa	Pacífico Norte	**9.** North Pacific
Europa	**3.** Europe	Pacífico Sur	**10.** South Pacific
Norteamérica	**4.** North America	Atlántico Norte	**11.** North Atlantic
Suramérica	**5.** South America	Atlántico Sur	**12.** South Atlantic
Australia	**6.** Australia	Indico	**13.** Indian
Antártica	**7.** Antarctica	Antártico	**14.** Antarctic

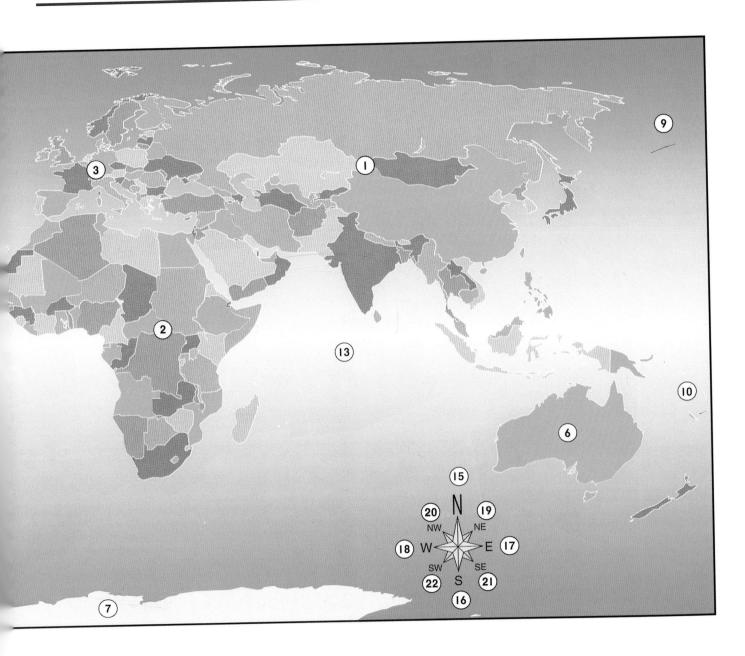

Orientaciones	**Directions**
norte	**15.** north
sur	**16.** south
este	**17.** east
oeste	**18.** west
noreste	**19.** northeast
noroeste	**20.** northwest
sureste	**21.** southeast
suroeste	**22.** southwest

Alabama	1. Alabama		Indiana	14. Indiana
Alaska	2. Alaska		Iowa	15. Iowa
Arizona	3. Arizona		Kansas	16. Kansas
Arkansas	4. Arkansas		Kentucky	17. Kentucky
California	5. California		Luisiana	18. Louisiana
Colorado	6. Colorado		Maine	19. Maine
Connecticut	7. Connecticut		Maryland	20. Maryland
Delaware	8. Delaware		Massachusetts	21. Massachusetts
Florida	9. Florida		Michigan	22. Michigan
Georgia	10. Georgia		Minesota	23. Minnesota
Hawaii	11. Hawaii		Misisipí	24. Mississipi
Idaho	12. Idaho		Misurí	25. Missouri
Illinois	13. Illinois		Montana	26. Montana

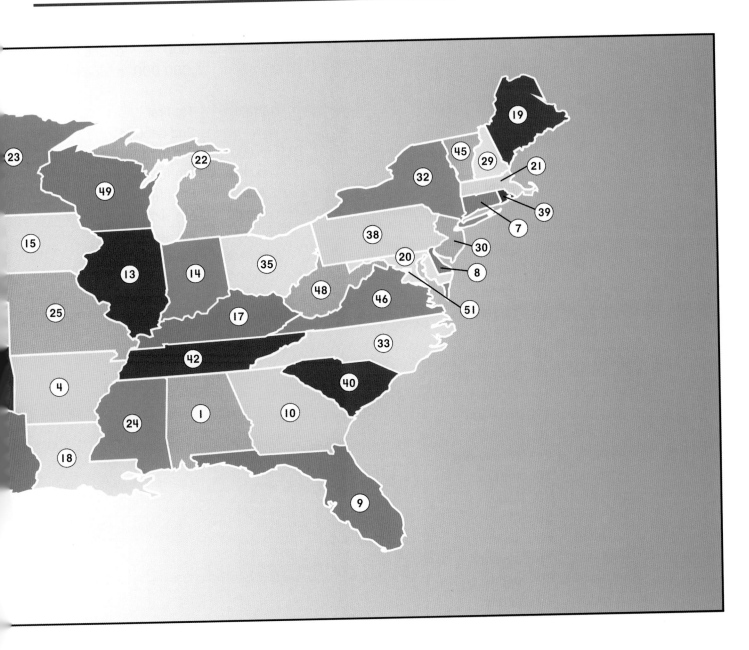

Nebraska	27. Nebraska	Carolina del Sur	40. South Carolina
Nevada	28. Nevada	Dakota del Sur	41. South Dakota
New Hampshire	29. New Hampshire	Tenesí	42. Tennessee
Nueva Jersey	30. New Jersey	Texas	43. Texas
Nuevo México	31. New Mexico	Utah	44. Utah
Nueva York	32. New York	Vermont	45. Vermont
Carolina del Norte	33. North Carolina	Virginia	46. Virginia
Dakota del Norte	34. North Dakota	Washington	47. Washington
Ohio	35. Ohio	Virginia Occidental	48. West Virginia
Oklahoma	36. Oklahoma	Wisconsin	49. Wisconsin
Oregón	37. Oregon	Wyoming	50. Wyoming
Pensilvania	38. Pennsylvania	Distrito de Columbia	51. District of Columbia
Rhode Island	39. Rhode Island		

uno	1	one
dos	2	two
tres	3	three
cuatro	4	four
cinco	5	five
seis	6	six
siete	7	seven
ocho	8	eight
nueve	9	nine
diez	10	ten
once	11	eleven
doce	12	twelve
trece	13	thirteen
catorce	14	fourteen
quince	15	fifteen
dieciséis	16	sixteen
diecisiete	17	seventeen
dieciocho	18	eighteen
diecinueve	19	nineteen
veinte	20	twenty
veintiuno	21	twenty-one
treinta	30	thirty
cuarenta	40	forty
cincuenta	50	fifty
sesenta	60	sixty
setenta	70	seventy
ochenta	80	eighty
noventa	90	ninety
cien/ciento	100	a/one hundred
quinientos	500	five hundred
seiscientos veintiuno	621	six hundred (and) twenty-one

mil	1,000	a/one thousand
un millón	1,000,000	a/one million

primero	1st first
segundo	2nd second
tercero	3rd third
cuarto	4th fourth
quinto	5th fifth
sexto	6th sixth
séptimo	7th seventh
octavo	8th eighth
noveno	9th ninth
décimo	10th tenth

Abreviaciones   Abbreviations

onzas	ounces	oz
cucharadita	teaspoon	tsp
cucharada	tablespoon	tbs
pinta	pint	pt
cuarto	quart	qt
galón	gallon	gal
libra(s)	pound(s)	lb(s)
pulgada	inch	in
pie / pies	foot / feet	ft
yarda(s)	yard(s)	yd(s)
milla	mile	mi

litro	liter	l
mililitro	milliliter	ml
gramo	gram	g
miligramo	milligram	mg
kilogramo	kilogram	kg
metro	meter	m
centímetro	centimeter	cm
kilómetro	kilometer	km

Longitud, altura y distancia   Length, Height, and Distance

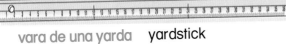

regla   ruler

vara de una yarda   yardstick

cinta de medir   measuring tape

1 ft	12 in
1 yd	3 ft
1 mi	1,760 yds

1 in	2.54 cm
1 ft	30.48 cm
1 yd	.941 m
1 mi	1.609 km

Medidas líquidas   Liquid Measure

cucharadita   teaspoon

cucharada   tablespoon

taza   cup

un cuarto de taza   a quarter cup

un tercio de taza   a third cup

media taza   a half cup

1 oz	29.6 ml
1 c	236.5 ml
1 pt	473 ml
1 qt	.946 l
1 / 2 gal	1.893 l
1 gal	3.786 l

1 tbs	3 tsp	1 / 2 oz
1 c	16 tbs	8 oz
1 pt	2 c	16 oz
1 qt	2 pt	32 oz
1 / 2 gal	2 qt	64 oz
1 gal	4 qt	128 oz

Pesos sólidos   Solid Weights

1 lb	454 g
1 kg	2.205 lbs

Abreviaciones   **Abbreviations**

grados Fahrenheit	degrees Fahrenheit	°F
grados Centígrados	degrees Celsius/centigrade	°C

From Fahrenheit to Celsius/Centigrade
De Fahrenheit a Centígrados

subtract 32, multiply by 5, divide by 9
reste 32, multiplique por 5, divida entre 9

50°F   50
         -32
          18 x 5 = 90

          90 ÷ 9 = 10°C

From Celsius/Centigrade to Fahrenheit
De Centígrados a Fahrenheit

multiply by 9, divide by 5, add 32
multiplique por 9, divida entre 5, sume 32

10°C   10 x 9 = 90

         90 ÷ 5 = 18
               +32
               50°F

Two numbers occur after words in the index: the first refers to the page where the word is illustrated and the second to the item number of the word on that page. For example, above [ə būv**'**] **54**/1 means that the word *above* is the item numbered 1 on page 54. If only a bold number appears, then that word is part of the unit title or a subtitle.

The index includes a pronunciation guide for all the words illustrated in the book. This guide uses symbols commonly found in dictionaries for native speakers. These symbols, unlike those used in transcription systems such as the International Phonetic Alphabet, tend to preserve spelling and so should help you to become more aware of the connections between written English and spoken English.

Consonants

[b] as in **back** [băk]   [k] as in **kiss** [kĭs]   [sh] as in **ship** [shĭp]
[ch] as in **cheek** [chēk]   [l] as in **leg** [lĕg]   [t] as in **tape** [tāp]
[d] as in **date** [dāt]   [m] as in **man** [măn]   [th] as in **three** [thrē]
[dh] as in **the** [dh]   [n] as in **neck** [nĕk]   [v] as in **vest** [vĕst]
[f] as in **face** [fās]   [ng] as in **ring** [rĭng]   [w] as in **waist** [wāst]
[g] as in **gas** [găs]   [p] as in **pack** [păk]   [y] as in **yard** [yärd]
[h] as in **half** [hăf]   [r] as in **rake** [rāk]   [z] as in **zip** [zĭp]
[j] as in **jeans** [jēnz]   [s] as in **sad** [săd]   [zh] as in **measure** [mĕzh**'**ər]

Vowels

[ā] as in **bake** [bāk]   [ī] as in **lime** [līm]   [ōō] as in **cool** [kōōl]
[ă] as in **back** [băk]   [ĭ] as in **lip** [lĭp]   [ŏŏ] as in **book** [bŏŏk]
[ä] as in **bar** [bär]   [ï] as in **heel** [hïl]   [ow] as in **brown** [brown]
[ē] as in **bean** [bēn]   [ō] as in **post** [pōst]   [oy] as in **boy** [boy]
[ĕ] as in **bed** [bĕd]   [ŏ] as in **box** [bŏks]   [ŭ] as in **cut** [kŭt]
[ë] as in **pear** [për]   [ö] as in **lawn** [lön]   [ü] as in **curb** [kürb]
                                    or **for** [för]   [ə] as in **above** [ə būv**'**]

All pronunciation symbols used are alphabetical except for the schwa [ə], which is the most frequent vowel sound in English. If you use it appropriately in unstressed syllables, your pronunciation will sound more natural.

You should note that an umlaut ([¨]) calls attention to the special quality of vowels before [r]. (The sound [ö] can also represent a vowel not followed by [r] as in *lawn*.) You should listen carefully to native speakers to discover how these vowels actually sound.

Stress

This guide also follows the system for marking stress used in many dictionaries for native speakers.
   (1) Stress is not marked if a word consisting of a single syllable occurs in isolation.
   (2) Where stress is marked, two levels are distinguished:
        a bold accent [**'**] is placed after each syllable with primary stress.
        a light accent [**'**] is placed after each syllable with secondary stress.

Syllable Boundaries

Syllable boundaries are indicated by a single space.

NOTE: The pronunciation used in this index is based on patterns of American English. There has been no attempt to represent all of the varieties of American English. Students should listen to native speakers to hear how the language actually sounds in a particular region.

MASTERING REAL ESTATE MATH

EIGHTH EDITION

Dearborn™
A Kaplan Real Estate Education Company

This publication is designed to provide accurate and authoritative information in regard to the subject matter covered. It is sold with the understanding that the publisher is not engaged in rendering legal, accounting, or other professional advice. If legal advice or other expert assistance is required, the services of a competent professional should be sought.

President: Dr. Andrew Temte
Chief Learning Officer: Dr. Tim Smaby
Vice President, Real Estate Education: Asha Alsobrooks
Development Editor: Adam Bissen

MASTERING REAL ESTATE MATH, EIGHTH EDITION
©2012 Kaplan, Inc.
Published by DF Institute, Inc., d/b/a Dearborn Real Estate Education
332 Front St. S., Suite 501
La Crosse, WI 54601

All rights reserved. The text of this publication, or any part thereof, may not be reproduced in any manner whatsoever without written permission from the publisher.

Printed in the United States of America
12   13   14   10   9   8   7   6   5   4   3   2   1
ISBN: 978-1-4277-3143-2 / 1-4277-3143-8
PPN: 1512-1008